THE NILE

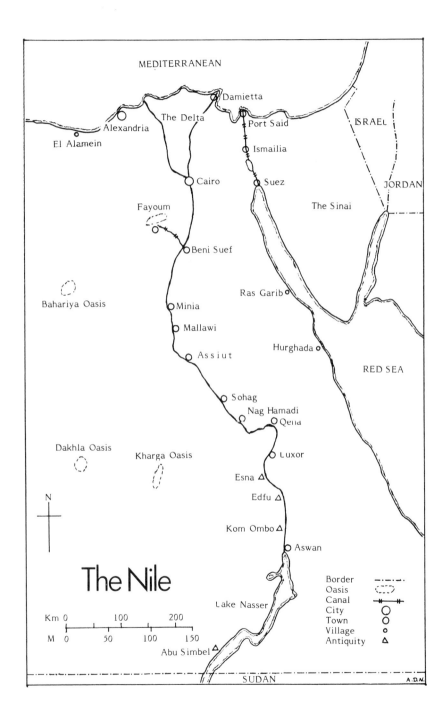

MEDITERRANEAN

Damietta

Alexandria

The Delta

Port Said

ISRAEL

El Alamein

Ismailia

Cairo

Suez

JORDAN

Fayoum

The Sinai

Beni Suef

Ras Garib

Bahariya Oasis

Minia

Mallawi

Hurghada

Assiut

RED SEA

Sohag

Nag Hamadi

Qena

Dakhla Oasis

Kharga Oasis

Luxor

Esna △

N

Edfu △

Kom Ombo △

Aswan

The Nile

Lake Nasser

| Km | 0 | | 100 | | 200 |
| M | 0 | 50 | 100 | | 150 |

Border
Oasis
Canal
City
Town
Village
Antiquity △

Abu Simbel △

SUDAN

A.D.N.

THE
NILE

NINA NELSON

B. T. BATSFORD LTD · LONDON

To Tony — also a devotee of Egypt

First Published 1986
© Nina Nelson 1986

ISBN 0 7134 46447

Typeset by SB Datagraphics Ltd
Printed in Great Britain by
Butler & Tanner Ltd
Frome, Somerset
for the publishers
B.T. Batsford Ltd
4 Fitzhardinge Street
London
W1H 0AH

Contents

Acknowledgements

The information on which to base a travel book can only be collected by research, both on the ground and in the relevant literature. This in turn is facilitated by officials, experts, friends and contacts. I have once again been most fortunate in my dealings with all these.

Sami el Masri, the knowledgeable Tourist Relations Director of EGAPT, pointed my efforts in all the right ways and smoothed my path. Samira Abdel Sayed, a great friend, and her husband, Yehia, made many unique suggestions including Dr Ragab's island. Siham Raouf, the Passenger Services Vice President of EgyptAir, brought my flights of fancy down to earth when necessary and helped with the recipes.

Ismail Shahin, Director of the Egyptian Tourist Office in London, produced useful information and made arrangements. My thanks also to Hosni Elsharif of the same office. Ted Woodhams of EgyptAir, London, knows Egypt inside out and was able to tell me what to avoid as well as what to do. He also compiled the list of Nile cruisers. Stephanie Goodenough, Managing Director of Egyptian Encounter, gave me a lot of up-to-date pointers.

In Egypt, willing assistance was provided by Ali Gohar, the broadcaster, Dr Salah Wahab, a lawyer and tourism expert and Tawfik Souidan who, when not practising as a surgeon, has an intimate knowledge of the night spots. Muktar Zaki, lately a diplomat and now using his skills in the hotel world, was most welcoming and, in Aswan, Ali Kahala was always on call. Much of the technical expertise on Egyptology was provided by Commander Amir Fouad, the lecturer on one of the cruises and Sonia, Sami el Masri's wife.

I know that I shall be indebted to my editor at Batsford, Simon Tuite, by the time this manuscript becomes a book. Finally, due to the marvels of modern technology, the manuscript more or less typed itself!

1

TRAVELLING IN EGYPT

Of the Nile's 4000 mile (6400 km) journey through the length of Africa, without doubt its greatest attraction today for the tourist is the 600 miles within Egypt. Probably no other stretch of river in the world has so many interesting features or enjoys so romantic a reputation. If while speeding along a noisy motorway you sometimes wonder what it would be like to slow down, dispel the clatter and actually enjoy the quietness of the countryside, one answer could be cruising on the Nile. Along this silent highway, merging with the usual river traffic, some 80 'floating hotels', varying in capacity from 20 to 200 passengers, thread their way back and forth between Cairo and Aswan.

Among the enticing reasons for such a holiday are the predictable sunny weather, the proximity of the antiquities to the river which, after all, brought them into existence, and the flat calm water which eliminates motion sickness. Perhaps the prime consideration is that, instead of constant re-packing and transfer to plane, train or bus, your accommodation accompanies you. Your guides, often well known Egyptologists, travel with you and brief you before going ashore for the day's sightseeing. The passing panorama as you cruise along is fascinating and soothing to nerves frayed by modern living. After an expedition ashore, it is pleasant to know that your next meal awaits your return in an air-conditioned dining room and should you be thirsty, a well-stocked bar is always open.

Egypt has been an alluring place since ancient times. Long before the turn-of-the-century's grand tour, the Greeks and Romans discovered it. In the Victorian era, river craft had oars as well as sails. One of the first requirements in those days when hiring a small boat and crew was to have it sunk to get rid of the rats before getting the provisions aboard. The most popular way to travel for Europeans was by *dahabeah*. This was an attractive vessel with lateen sails and hand-carved wooden sides and stairways. The sharp prow and broad stern made a romantic sight, especially when gliding along in the moonlight. How astonished the Victorians would be today to find air-conditioned rooms instead of cabins, and windows instead of portholes. Top decks no longer boast sails but swimming pools, areas for sun-tanning, games, a bar and café. Stainless steel kitchens with deep freezers and refrigerators have replaced the old galleys. The skipper has been rechristened the Captain Manager. (A list of Nile cruise ships and hotels will be found at the end of the book).

One of Sheraton's Nile cruise ships

Two sights which our forebears would be glad not to see are crocodiles basking on the banks and the obligatory visit to a slave market. Though the latter were of course universally condemned, they seem to have been an unavoidable exhibit. Happily, neither exist any longer. However, many of the scenes along the Nile are still the same as delighted Anthony and Cleopatra. The great monuments, temples and fantastic tombs have lost nothing of their grandeur. The lateen sails of the feluccas, the famous river sailing-boats, are still hoisted by men who wear the same type of long cotton robe and skull cap as their ancestors. Peasants, the fellaheen, till the soil with oxen, water-buffaloes turn water-wheels and camels edge the skyline on the way to market. Women draw water from the river in large clay pots which they balance on their heads. Somehow the ancient mixes with the modern in the same sharp contrast as the desert does with the delta. In the townships and villages, horsedrawn gharries (carriages) are passed by taxis and buses, boys wearing jeans ride by on donkeys while others in long robes, the galabia, speed along on motor cycles. Washing hangs on balconies next to office blocks, mosque

A smaller Nile cruiser belonging to Abercrombie & Kent

minarets vie with high-rise office buildings. Muslim and Christian communities mingle and festivals are legion. It is all a mixture but exhilarating.

To enhance a stay in Egypt it is useful to have some knowledge of the customs of the people, what to pack, the weather, and what to expect.

Climate

The weather is almost 100% predictable. If you arrange to go sightseeing, on a picnic or travel somewhere, you can count on a sunny day and a clear cool night even during the winter. Spring (March to May) and autumn (September to November) are the seasons Americans and Europeans seem to enjoy most, when the climate is nearest to their ideal. Winter has always been a favourite time as it is crisp, cool and sunny. The least popular time is summer when it can be very hot–but this does not apply so much today with universal air conditioning. Wind storms called khamseens occur about five or six times a year. These hot, gusty winds pick up the desert sand and carry it everywhere like a giant sand-blasting machine, blotting out sun and sky. Fortunately they do not last long, and it is best to stay in your cabin or hotel room if possible until the sky clears. Another point to remember is that temperatures drop sharply at night.

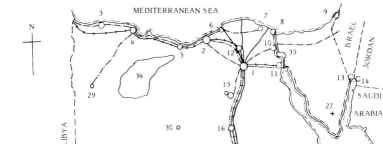

KEY
1 Cairo
2 Alexandria
3 Sidi Barrani
4 Mersa Matruh
5 El Alamein
6 Rosetta
7 Damietta
8 Port Said
9 Gaza
10 Ismailia
11 Suez
12 Tanta
13 Eilat
14 Aqaba
15 Fayoum
16 El Minya
17 Assiut
18 Qena
19 Luxor
20 Aswan
21 Wadi Halfa
22 Hurgada
23 Esna
24 Edfu
25 Kom Ombo
26 Abu Simbel
27 St Catherine's Monast
28 Lake Nasser
29 Siwa Oasis
30 Bahariya Oasis
31 Dakla Oasis
32 Farafra Oasis
33 El Kharga Oasis
34 Quattara Depression
35 Suez Canal

Mean maximum air temperature. Centigrade

	Cairo	Alexandria	Luxor	Aswan
Jan	19.1	18.3	23.0	23.8
Feb	20.7	19.2	25.4	26.1
Mar	23.7	21.0	29.0	30.4
Apr	28.2	23.6	34.8	35.0
May	32.4	26.5	39.3	38.5
Jun	34.5	28.2	40.7	42.1
Jul	35.4	29.6	40.8	41.2
Aug	33.8	30.4	41.0	41.3
Sep	32.3	29.4	38.5	39.6
Oct	29.8	27.7	35.1	36.3
Nov	25.1	24.4	29.6	30.2
Dec	20.7	20.4	24.8	25.5

Mean minimum air temperature. Centigrade

	Cairo	Alexandria	Luxor	Aswan
Jan	8.6	9.3	5.4	8.0
Feb	9.3	9.7	6.8	9.4
Mar	11.3	11.2	10.7	12.6
Apr	13.9	13.5	15.7	17.5
May	17.4	16.7	20.7	21.1
Jun	17.9	20.2	22.6	24.2

	Cairo	Alexandria	Luxor	Aswan
Jul	21.5	22.7	23.6	24.5
Aug	21.6	22.9	23.5	24.7
Sep	19.9	21.3	21.5	22.2
Oct	17.8	17.8	17.8	19.3
Nov	13.9	14.8	12.2	14.5
Dec	10.4	11.2	7.7	9.9

What to pack

Advice is difficult because there are so many personal things that must be taken. However, in general, clothes that would be worn during spring and autumn at home, are suitable for the winter. A wool sweater, cardigan or light anorak is useful and perhaps a light coat. Low walking shoes are a must but not sandals as they let in the sand. Binoculars, even small ones, are worthwhile, especially when gliding along the Nile or seeing views from temples and high buildings. Incidentally, they are still one of the things you can carry during air travel. Sunglasses are essential and if you have no room for a sun-hat, they can be bought cheaply anywhere. Lipsalve is useful. It is very important to carry a good torch. The monuments are sometimes ill lit inside and, although guides carry them, if you wish to see something special or return for a second look at a mural, you need your own light.

Photography

Egypt is a photographer's paradise and you certainly should bring your own camera and flash. It is perhaps best to have your own film of the type you know, though you can buy films locally. Photography is prohibited in some places but these are clearly marked, such as bridges, dams, ports, airports and restricted areas. Many of the country folk do not wish to be photographed but if you ask them first, sometimes they will agree.

Health

It is essential to check with your doctor or chemist about injections and pills to take in case of stomach upset. In a hot climate, food deteriorates quickly and it is wise not to buy from street stalls. Hotels and restaurants are usually extremely careful but an odd fly can spell disaster. You will find more information in the food and drink chapter. You can obtain advice on injections from the centres operated by British Airways or Thomas Cook or, of course, from your own doctor.

Water

It is important nowadays to drink bottled water–available everywhere–rather than from the tap. It was not always so but the great influx of people since the oil boom, the Middle East wars and the catastrophe in the Lebanon, has increased the population by millions and greatly overloaded the water distribution system. Try not to take ice with your drinks, unless you are certain it has been made with bottled or purified water.

Arrival
Both EgyptAir and British Airways have daily direct flights from London and TWA from New York. As well as passports, visas are required by all nationalities. All personal effects, used or new, including cameras, radios, typewriters, tape–or video–recorders and jewelry are exempt from customs duties and other taxes, provided they are listed on a declaration form. The original is kept by the Customs Office and a stamped copy is retained by the visitor until departure. Alcohol, tobacco and medicines of less value than twenty Egyptian pounds are exempt.

Currency
Egyptian currency may not be taken into or out of the country. Visitors must exchange a minimum of the equivalent of £100 on arrival. The unit of currency is the Egyptian pound, abbreviated L.E., which is subdivided into 100 piastres. As the exchange rate will be out of date by the time this is published, it is not quoted here. It is advisable to ignore the illegal black market. Bank note denominations are 100, 20, 10, 5 and 1; piastres 50, 25, 10 and 5. Coins are 10, 5, 1 and 1/2 piastre. Banks are generally open 09:30–12:30 Monday to Thursday and Saturday, 10:30–12:30 Sunday, and closed Friday. Hotels will cash travellers cheques.

Tipping
A small tip, or 'baksheesh', is always expected for every service. Always try to get small change from your bank or hotel as, for some reason, nobody ever seems to have any.

Shops
These are usually open from 9 a.m. to 8 p.m. in summer and 10 a.m. to 7 p.m. in winter.

Tourist offices
The head office in Cairo is at 5 Adly Street. Each town has its own office. There is an organization called the Tourist Police who are trained to help tourists. They wear dark blue uniforms with silver buttons and you will find them at stations, airports, sightseeing places, museums and markets.

Taxis
Most taxis are fitted with meters. Many drivers will forget to switch on the meter and it is best to agree the fare before taking a cab. In the case of wireless-fitted airport limousines, the fare is fixed for given distances.

Self-Drive hire cars
These are available and several of the international companies such as Hertz and Avis are represented. There are however two factors which should give food for thought before you hire. First of all driving, especially in Cairo, can be

On deck aboard an Abercrombie & Kent cruise ship

a unique experience. Do not imagine that, because you are happy in London, Paris or Rome, you will understand Egyptian driving habits. Secondly, remember that unless you speak and read Arabic, navigation can prove frustrating.

Electricity
Most of Egypt is 220 volt AC. Be prepared for power cuts.

Distances
A few distances will give you an idea of the scale of the country.

From Cairo by road to:	Miles	Km
El Alamein	190	304
Alexandria	140	224
Assiut	235	376
Aswan	550	880
Fayoum	65	104
Luxor	420	672
Port Said	135	216
Suez	245	392

Internal travel
EgyptAir operates several daily services between Cairo, Luxor, Aswan and Abu Simbel. There are twice weekly flights to Hurghada on the Red Sea. The rail trip from Cairo to Alexandria takes $2\frac{3}{4}$ hours, to Luxor 12 hours and to Aswan 16 hours. Night trains are equipped with comfortable sleepers where meals are brought to you as in an aircraft. There are also restaurant cars and piped music if you wish it. There is a regular bus service between Cairo International Airport and the city centre. Contact the tourist office at the airport for information. There are also bus services between the main cities.

Bargaining
This has always been a feature of shopping but is more usually encountered nowadays in stalls, markets and frontless shops. Most large stores, hotel and government shops have prices clearly marked in Arabic numerals. As you only have to memorize ten figures and they are also useful for bus and house numbers, it is worthwhile trying to learn them. Here they are.

Number	Phonetic	Arabic
1	Wahid	١
2	Eckneen	٢
3	Talata	٣
4	Arba	٤
5	Khamsa	٥
6	Sitta	٦
7	Sarba	٧
8	Tamanya	٨
9	Tessa	٩
10	Ashra	١٠

Newspapers
There are two English papers: the *Egyptian Mail* and the *Egyptian Gazette*, the latter established in 1880. There are also booklets issued to hotels for visitors called *This Week in Cairo* and *This Week in Alexandria* which are in English and French and tell you what is going on during the forthcoming week.

Television and radio
As well as Arabic programmes, there are American and English shows so you can sometimes keep up-to-date with your favourite serials in your hotel room. There are several news bulletins in English on TV and radio, the best known news reader being Ali Gohar. You can check the times in your newspaper which is often delivered gratis with your hotel breakfast.

Useful addresses
British Embassy: 2 Ahmed Raghab St, Garden City, Tel. 20850. Australian Embassy: 1097, Cornich el-Nil St, Garden City, Tel. 28190. Canadian

Embassy: 6 Mohammed Fahmy es Sayed, Garden City, Tel. 23110. American Embassy: 5 Latin America St, Garden City, Tel. 28219.

Dynasties, Gods and Goddesses

Dynasties, Gods and Goddesses
The Egyptians recorded their history in dynasties some thirty centuries before the Roman Conquest, each being a line of hereditary pharaohs. A famous tablet at Abydos temple fortunately gives a list of 75 of these rulers starting with Mena, 4400 B.C. and going to Seti the First, 1300 B.C. It is believed by several historians that the latter was the Pharaoh responsible in the Bible for the exodus of the Jews from Egypt.

The dynasties have been divided into three periods known as the Ancient Empire (11 dynasties), the Middle Kingdom (9 dynasties) and the New Kingdom (10 dynasties). Then came the rule of the Persians, Macedonians, Ptolemies and Romans followed by the Arab conquest in 641 A.D. During dynastic times, the arts flourished and were held in esteem second only to the Pharaoh himself. Temples, statues and carvings reached a peak of perfection not known before. For those who wrote the papyrus documents, the mere signature 'Scribe' was held in as much veneration as such signatures as Rembrandt, Rubens and Vermeer were to achieve thousands of years later.

Today we can still enjoy and marvel at the treasures of Ancient Egypt. Temple carvings and murals can be enjoyed just because they are beautiful, but to distinguish the various gods and goddesses is often difficult. Certainly their history reads like the Greek myths. Ra was the self-begotten Sun God, also known as Amen-Ra. His son Osiris married Isis, Goddess of the Earth, later of the Moon. Osiris was hated and murdered by his brother Set, Prince of Darkness. Osiris was resurrected and he and Isis begot Horus who became Lord of the Earth while Osiris took over as God of the Underworld and Judge of the Dead.

During religious ceremonies, priests would put on animal masks when representing gods for each god possessed not only all the virtues of the human but also characteristics attributed to an animal or bird. Thus Sekmet the God of War had the strength of a lion and so wore a lion's head. Anubis had the jackal's head, signifying its speed. Horus had the keen sight of the hawk so he wore the hawk's head. The following short list gives the name of the favourite symbol associated with some of the better known deities.

Amen-Ra	hawk and ram
Anubis	jackal
Bast	cat
Hathor	cow
Horus	hawk
Khnum	ram
Mut	vulture
Ptah	bull
Thoth	ibis

A twin-masted felucca with a cargo of quarried stone

As will be noted, many symbols are repeated and there is much room for confusion but the visitor may begin to understand the pictorial writing on the temple walls with a little practice. For instance, gods and goddesses can be recognized by their head-dresses. Emblems of rule, sovereignty and dominion are the crook, the sceptre and the flail.

Today's Egyptian

For centuries, the Egyptian has had foreigners on his soil. Napoleon and Nelson vied with each other. De Lesseps brought the Suez canal into existence, the British used Egypt as a base during the two world wars. The Russians helped to build the High Dam at Aswan.

In 1953 Egypt became a republic and regained its national identity. Tourism has always been one of the main sources of income but this was bedevilled latterly by the Middle East wars. However, the Camp David agreement signed by Egypt's President Sadat and Israel's Prime Minister Begin, under the auspices of US President Carter in 1979, has produced some stability and tourism is once again a major pillar of the Egyptian economy.

The visitor will soon notice that the Muslim faith is one of the cornerstones of Egyptian life. Five times a day, the call to prayer rings out from the minarets and your taxi driver may well excuse himself for a few minutes while he leaves you to make his obeisances facing Mecca. Friday is the Muslim Sunday, when all government offices and shops are closed.

Ramadan is to the Muslim what Lent is to the Christian, only far more stringent. It begins when the new moon rises in the ninth month of the Muslim year and from then a strict fast from dawn to dusk is observed for twenty-eight days. Small children, the sick and old people are excused and there are certain other dispensations, including travellers. When booking a holiday, it is wise to find out when Ramadan falls. This varies annually as the Muslim calendar does not coincide with ours. If it occurs during the heat of the summer, the strict provision that no water may be drunk during the daylight hours imposes considerable discomfort on the faithful. Service in hotels tends to suffer to some extent but it is less noticeable during a winter Ramadan.

The Copts are a Christian community in Egypt who exert considerable influence. They originally had their own language but this is now used only for liturgical purposes. In 64 A.D. Saint Mark ordained Ananius Patriarch of Alexandria and the city became a Christian centre. Two hundred years later, Saint Anthony withdrew from Alexandria to the desert to abstain from worldly things. There he taught his Christian followers to lead an ascetic life and so started the first monastery.

The Copts are not subject to Rome but do have confession which is obligatory before receiving the Eucharist. During services, the clergy and choir occupy that part of the church containing the altar, the male congregation sit in a second section and the women sit by themselves in a third enclosure. Screens separate the sections.

Both Muslims and Christians believe in one God and share many prophets. Much of the Koran is similar to the Bible. After all, Moses was found in the bullrushes by Pharaoh's daughter! However, there are two obvious differences. The Christian, except in church, prefers to worship in private whereas the Muslim will go down on his knees—with or without a prayer mat—wherever he happens to be at the time and whether he is observed or not. The contrast is in the attitude towards cemeteries. Christian cemetaries sometimes suffer from neglect while Muslim ones often resemble small villages. Graves with white or pastel coloured domes are well kept and families go on special occasions to eat and be happy thinking of departed relatives.

Some Festivals

The delightful reason for Shem el Nessim is to celebrate the first day of spring. It is a national holiday. The name means 'smell the breeze' and it is fixed by the Coptic calendar for the Monday following Easter Sunday. It is not a religious holiday and everyone, regardless of creed, joins in. Jewelry and new or best clothes are worn and people parade in parks and gardens.

Maulid el Nabi (the birthday of the prophet Muhammad) is also a national holiday and, with its many charming and picturesque customs, is one of the happiest festivals of the year. Preparations for it start some weeks in advance and gaily decorated stalls appear in the market place with rows of white sugar dolls clad in coloured paper dresses. The actual celebration does not begin until the eve of the feast. Members of the Soofi orders march through the streets carrying banners with quotations from the Koran. Later they perform the mystical rite of the Zikr or Turning, which carries on into the small hours. Marquees are put up where singers recall old Islamic tales accompanied by reed instruments, poets recite, and there are readings from the Prophets life. Those who prefer to stay in their own homes for the feasts can listen to the radio. As darkness falls, the minarets are lit up so that in Cairo, from the tower, it looks as though countless jewelled bracelets are suspended above the city.

The most important holiday during the year is at the end of Ramadan (the month of fasting) which is called Bairam and lasts three days. It is similar to Christmas in that families and friends exchange gifts. New clothes are obtained and parties planned. Decorated cakes and sweetmeats appear.

Besides the religious occasions, there are sporting festivals such as golf, tennis, yacht-racing, water-skiing and an Arabian horse festival. Whatever season of the year, no matter what is going on, of one thing the tourist can be sure: he will be met with a ready smile and friendly greeting. *Ahlen wiz ahlen.* Welcome, thrice welcome.

2

CAIRO

TWA flies direct from New York, EgyptAir or British Airways straight from London, but you will often arrive after dark at Cairo airport. On leaving the aircraft, a feeling of well being creeps over you due to the warm dry air. Should you gaze up at the sky, the stars seem much closer because of the clear atmosphere. If you did not purchase your duty free allowances before starting your flight or on the aircraft, you are not too late to do so, because you can visit the duty free shop before going through customs, a facility not available at many airports.

The airport is some 12 miles (20 km) from the city centre and, after collecting your luggage, you are soon on your way by bus or taxi, driving along a dual carriageway. Depending on your destination in the city, you will drive on elevated roadways, bridges across the Nile and through large midans or squares. Bright lights and gaudy neon signs are everywhere and traffic lights flash red and green, though often ignored! At night the streets are less congested than by day, when monumental traffic jams can occur. Should you pass a huge statue, it will be that of Ramses II in front of the main railway station. It was carved out of a monolithic granite block, weighs some eighty tons and has a fountain in front of it. It was brought from Memphis where it once stood before the temple of Ptah. The great head looks over the surrounding buildings towards the Nile, the river where far away at Abu Simbel, four other statues of the Pharaoh gaze across the water in the same contemplative way.

In Cairo, the Nile is the main thoroughfare. Skyscraper hotels with familiar names like Sheraton, Hilton, Intercontinental and Shepheards, pierce the night sky, their lighted windows reflected in the shiny black water. The Cairo Tower, soaring some 600 feet, or 185 metres, casts its own reflection right across to the opposite side in an attractive lacy pattern, for about 12 million pieces of pottery make up its perforated design. Rows of golden street lights line each bank, joined together here and there by those on the bridges. Along the banks you can discern feluccas tied up for the night. Tiny dots of red on the decks, show where the crews are cooking their evening meal.

In the daytime you have a clear view from rooftop restaurants or skyscraper rooms and can quickly get an idea of the layout of the city. Part of it is built on two islands in the river, Gezira (meaning island) and Roda, which are

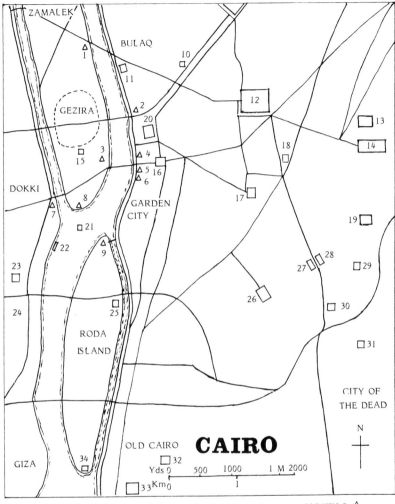

PLACES OF INTEREST □
10 Offices of Al Ahram
11 TV Studios
12 Ezbekiya Gardens
13 Khan el Khalili
14 Al Azhar Mosque & University
15 Cairo Tower
16 Tahrir Square
17 Abdin Palace
18 Museum of Islamic Art
19 Blue Mosque
20 Egyptian Antiquities Museum
21 Fountain

22 Papyrus Institute
23 Botanical Gardens
24 Zoological Gardens
25 Manial Palace Museum
26 Ibn Tulun Mosque
27 Sultan Husein Mosque
28 Rifei Mosque
29 Citadel
30 Mohammed Ali Mosque
31 Tombs of the Mamelukes
32 Fustat Ruins
33 Coptic Museum & St George's Church
34 Nilometer

HOTELS △
1 Marriott
2 Ramses Hilton
3 El Borg
4 Nile Hilton
5 Intercontinental
6 Shepheards
7 Sheraton
8 Sheraton Tower
9 Meridien

connected by bridges. Many of the embassies are in Garden City, which also has attractive villas and blocks of luxury flats. From here, a tree-lined corniche road leads out to Maadi, with its pleasant flats, villas and riverside restaurants. Then on to Helwan about 18 miles or 30 km distant, long ago known as a spa but now busy and industrialized. However, there is a Japanese garden and the Cabritage, where health-giving sulphur baths can be taken in the pool and there is still a treatment centre.

From the same height, you can glimpse mosques and slender minarets and in the far distance the Mokattam Hills, which act as a backdrop to the Muhammad Ali mosque. Its four identical minarets contrast with those of the great university and mosque of Al Azhar, and the stark solidarity of the Citadel.

Tahrir (meaning liberation) Square is the largest in Cairo, a sea of frantic traffic confounded by seemingly endless civil engineering works, amongst them a station for the new underground railway. You can cross the square on elevated pedestrian walkways and look down on the melee below. Roads lead off in many directions; Talaat Harb, Kasr el Nil and El Bustaan. The shopping district is nearby. Ezbekiya Gardens and Opera Square are a mile away to the east.

One of the delights of Opera Square was its Renaissance style opera house built by Khedive Ismail in 1869 to celebrate the completion of the Suez Canal. Emperors, kings, presidents and heads of state have attended performances there but sadly it was destroyed by fire in October 1971. Plans are afoot to rebuild it.

Cairo is fascinating for the variety it offers. You can step from an air-conditioned bus after a delicious gourmet meal into a museum with antiquities thousands of years old. If you begin to flag, you can return to your hotel, go shopping, play golf, go horse riding or perhaps take a sail on the Nile to watch the sunset. Your hotel porter can arrange whatever you wish. Mark Twain recalls in his *Innocents Abroad* his pleasure at changing pursuits, but his transport was the humble donkey. He enjoyed the cool breezes as they raced, the palm fringed gardens, the black shadows of the trees at sunset and the Nile, silver when they reached it at the end of the day. There they dismounted, boarded a felucca together with donkey boys and donkeys, and went sailing. As in Mark Twain's case, it is nice to know that anything you miss in Cairo on the outward journey, can be seen conveniently on your return there at the end of your visit.

There are two Hilton hotels in Cairo, both on the east bank. The Ramses and the older Nile Hilton built in 1959, which has a most enviable site. It faces the Nile, backs onto Tahrir Square and to one side of it stands the Egyptian Antiquities Museum. Its main shop, Miss Egypt, is well known for its handbags and couture dresses. It has a rooftop nightclub and beyond its row of lobby shops, there is a swimming pool. The hotel is within walking distance of both the British and American embassies.

Egyptian Antiquities Museum

This is the richest museum of Egyptian antiquities in the world. It contains Pharaonic treasures covering 5000 years and is open daily from 9 a.m. until 4 p.m. and 9 a.m. until 11 a.m. on Fridays.

In 1850, a French Egyptologist, Francois Auguste Mariette, was sent to Cairo as an official of the Louvre. He was a devotee of Egyptology and luck seemed to be continually with him. His excavations were extremely fruitful and he was authorized to dig at Memphis, Giza—where he uncovered the body of the Sphinx—Meydun, Abydos and Karnak. His finds were so rewarding that, on the instructions of the Khedive Ismail, he was made founder of a new museum at Bulaq, which formed the basis of the one you see today. However, the discoveries have so increased in number and continue to do so today, that even the present edifice is too small and a further one is planned.

Mariette's archaeological knowledge was sought by the Khedive for yet another reason. He was asked to write the book of the opera which Verdi had been commissioned to compose for the opening of the Suez Canal. The result was *Aida* and authentic exhibits were lent from the museum for the first stage production.

Cairo Museum of Antiquities

The present museum is a rectangular building with a great rotunda on the ground floor as well as galleries and rooms lit by large skylights. Some of the exhibits are massive and the best views of them can be obtained looking down from upper galleries. A catalogue with reference numbers is of course available and it is easy to locate and identify the items which interest you.

The collection of royal mummies is displayed with dignity. It is difficult to understand how these frail remnants of human beings have survived their ordeal of movement since they were originally created. Hidden in shafts from tomb robbers, taken to museums for exhibition and, strangest of all, carried away by military ambulance. In the last world war a British Egyptologist, Brian Emery, then serving as a captain in Cairo, feared that, if the city was bombed, they could be lost for ever. He knew a rich old pasha who had built himself an elaborate tomb in his own garden in the suburbs. He eventually persuaded the pasha to allow the tomb to be used for the safe storage of the mummies. They were conveyed from the museum in military ambulances at the dead of night. They spent the rest of the war there though, in the event, Cairo was never bombed.

There is a special atmosphere in the museum and many books have been written about the amazing exhibits. Those in glass cases are displayed on white linen, a material always associated with ancient Egypt. After the noise in Tahrir Square, it seems strangely quiet, and there are more beautiful golden objects to be seen in Tutankhamun's gallery than anywhere else in the world. Since Howard Carter discovered them in the early twenties, nothing has vanished except a gilded walking stick, which was eventually found having fallen behind an exhibition case.

The Pharaoh had a collection of ceremonial sticks, two of them with interesting handles. One depicts an African and the other an Asian–both adversaries of Egypt at that time. At the entrance of this gallery there are two identical statues of the Pharaoh. The handsome figures have golden brows and eyelashes. They are clothed in golden skirts, sandals and necklaces. Their left feet are forward and the right arms held as if welcoming people. They were found thus at the entrance of the tomb.

Just a few feet beyond the entrance in the centre of the floor, is the golden shrine on which lies the famous jackal statue of Anubis, God of the Dead. He rests like the Giza Sphinx, paws forward, haunches close to his side but, unlike the Sphinx's curling tail, his hangs down at the back of the shrine. He is alert, and you can see daylight between the shrine and his haunches. The whites of his far-seeing eyes are visible, the gold lined ears stiffly upright and he has a golden ribbon falling down his chest. This masterpiece has never left Egypt, even when the Tutankhamun exhibitions were sent abroad in recent years. He is so thin that his rib cage shows through and it is interesting that, when Carter first found the tomb, a shawl was tied about his shoulders to ward off the cold.

The splendour of Pharaonic life is well displayed. Gilded furniture of every kind, chairs, divans, beds and most important of all, the magnificent gold-plated throne with decorative animal heads. At the back there is a carving depicting his Queen placing a necklace about the Pharaoh's shoulder. Cases of small golden figures show scenes of court life and hunting. Other cases contain exquisite ornaments and toilet requisites, such as a perfume box in the shape of a girl swimming and a mirror case designed like the Key of Life, inlaid with gems. But all are as nothing beside the famous golden mask. It is made of blue enamel, gold and lapis lazuli. The expression shows beneficence and tranquillity unexpected in a face so young, for the king died at the age of eighteen.

At the end of the gallery is a small room which houses the kings jewelry, a sumptuous array of semi-precious gems, turquoise, lapis, lazuli and cornelian. Long heavy earrings lie beside necklaces and collars of studded silver, scarabs, rings, anklets, bracelets and even gold finger sheaths.

There are so many different rooms and galleries in the museum that the half-day allotted on most tours is scarcely enough. For those interested in the Pyramids of Giza, in room 42 in the west gallery there is the seated figure of Chephren who built the second Pyramid. This was discovered in 1858 by Mariette. The famous seated Sakkara scribe is on the ground floor, his right hand poised above his tablet about to write. He looks thoughtfully beyond you. Several Pharaonic scribe statues have found their way into museums around the world, but this particular one seems alive and about to speak at any moment. Of the very small exhibits, there are several of Nile boats, none more attractive than the three discovered in Meketre's tomb in the Valley of the Nobles. One has a furled sail and the other two are fishing boats dragging a net between them. Once seen, who could forget the baby faience hippopotamus with painted lotus buds on chin and sides where one tiny bird has alighted on a stem. It is not surprising that people visit this museum again and again.

When you are leaving the museum you will notice that, to one side of the main entrance, there is a shop called 'Onnig of Cairo', a cafeteria and a branch of the National Bank where you can change money. If you miss the shop on arrival, look for it when you leave. Onnig is a famous jeweller who not only has replicas of treasures seen in the galleries, but also papyrus paintings and all kinds of Egyptian handicrafts. You may have seen his Pharaonic jewelry at the British Museum in London or the United Nations building in New York. He is a member of the American Gemmological Society. In his office are many photographs taken with famous personalities, but his greatest delight is in showing fellow Rotarians his collection of banners from all around the world.

Onnig designs the most intricate pieces of jewelry and will copy any design of your own. He does a very popular range of pendants. These are in the form of gold or silver cartouches on which he can have your name inscribed in hieroglyphics within the day.

Like most well known jewellers, Onnig has many fascinating tales to tell about his profession, and one concerns an Egyptian crown. As has been stated

Mask of Tutankhamun in Cairo Museum

earlier, Verdi wrote the opera *Aida* to celebrate the opening of the Suez Canal. The first performance in the Cairo Opera House was on Christmas Eve 1871. Under Mariette's guidance, part of Thebes was recreated on the stage, real Nubian slaves were used in the cast and a splendid crown was made by Parisian craftsmen for Aida to wear. The settings and costumes, kept down the years, were destroyed by the fire but Onnig had a replica of the crown on display in his shop in the old Semiramis hotel. Later he lent it to the New York Metropolitan Opera for use in their production of *Aida*. He now intends to present it to the new Cairo Opera House when it is built. It is notable that the Italians were so pleased with *Aida* when it was first presented at La Scala in Milan, that Verdi was given an ivory baton with 'Aida' inscribed on it in rubies.

Old Cairo

Old Cairo lies beyond the Garden City, southward on the way to Maadi on the east bank of the Nile, abreast of the lower end of Roda Island. It has a long history and has been much rebuilt. When the Persians conquered Egypt in the fifth century B.C. they made it their capital and named it Babel. Centuries later, after the Romans had built and rebuilt fortifications there, the Emperor Trajan (130 A.D.) named it Babylon. Finally the Christian Emperor Arcadius (395–408 B.C.) restored what was to become a great fortress covering about $\frac{1}{3}$ of a square mile (1 sq. km). During those days, the Egyptians had already been converted to Christianity. There was a river port 20 feet (6 m) below the present level of the streets and the Nile has since changed its course. It is here today that you will find some of the oldest churches in Christendom.

Al Muqallaqah is also known as the Hanging Church because it is built over one of the fortress towers. It remained the Patriarchal seat from the eleventh century when this was moved from Alexandria until the fourteenth century, so it is one of the most ancient churches in Egypt. The twelfth-century pulpit in the central nave rests on thirteen slender columns; six pairs stand behind a granite one representing Christ. Each pair is identical but no two pairs are alike, except for one painted black identified with Judas. Ikons of the Virgin and St Mark have trays of sand before them full of lighted candles. The pews are decorated at the back with fine hand-carved fretwork. A winding stairway leads up to a small chapel. Outside the church there are two rows of date palms in a tiny garden. They are similar to those from which the Holy Family ate dates while on their flight. Tradition has it that the mark on the stone was first left by the Virgin Mary when she bit into a date and stones have retained this mark ever since. Another charming story concerns what is known as the 'Virgins Tree' at Matariyah in Heliopolis. It is supposed to grow over the spot where the Holy Family rested during their journey.

Dating back to the eighth and ninth centuries stands the church of St Sergius, built over the middle of the fortress. No one knows who the saint was or anything about him. The church itself is very famous because of its crypt

The Coptic Church of St Sergius in Old Cairo, where the Holy Family are thought to have rested in a cave

which goes back to the fifth century and is believed to have been the site of a cave where the Holy Family stayed for thirty days.

St Sergius church is very small and a tiny dome over the altar is draped with embroidered curtains. If you get a chance to pull them aside, you can see the altar and sometimes a priest on the far side. Wooden bannisters edge the steps leading down to the crypt beyond. You can walk by the left side of the altar through an archway to reach the flight of steps. The space around them is quite empty and people quietly come and go after glancing down into the darkness. On my last visit, I was unable to go down into the crypt because of flooding. On a previous occasion I was able to see it. The chamber is quite small and contains some old marble columns and an altar in a wall recess.

Close by St Sergius church is that of St Barbara. Built in the eighth century, it has a reliquary containing a bone of the saint and a small chapel dedicated to St George. To the right of it is the Ben Ezra synagogue which you reach by a garden path lined with trees. It is very small and has some ancient Jewish scriptures or *torahs*. Originally it was a Coptic church but it was renamed after Rabbi Abraham Ben Ezra who bought it from the Copts in the twelfth century.

Another building over a bastion of the old fortress is the convent of St George. Round in design it is again very small but with disproportionately high ceiling and doorways, the entrance being eight metres high with suitably large hinges and locks on the door. Outside the crenellated walls surrounding the church have been restored recently.

According to legend, though without documentary proof, a Capadocian officer of the Roman Empire called George was put to death on the orders of Emperor Diocletian for publicly proclaiming his Christian faith. He was later beatified and churches of many Christian denominations throughout the Middle East were named after him. There has always been doubt as to whether he actually existed and Pope John XXIII decided formally in 1969 that he did not. However he remains popular and is remembered on 23rd April each year in Old Cairo when the church is crowded with pilgrims. A silver filigree framed ikon of the saint is believed to have curative powers and money left beneath it goes to the poor. It is said that, should a coin stick to the protective glass, your prayer will be granted. Visitors are also shown a great handful of clanking chains which are believed to have bound the saint before he was martyred.

It sometimes suprises tourists that these unique old churches have no organs. The music accompanying services is only by cymbals and tinkling brass bells. The latter are struck with tiny rods held in one hand. There are no images and only a few paintings. However, there are many ikons in Byzantine style. In early Christian times when churches were often attacked and the faithful had to flee, ikons were easy to carry and hide. Modern Coptic churches are similar to those of other creeds and there is a large new Coptic cathedral in central Cairo.

Before leaving Old Cairo, you must visit the Coptic Museum, part of which is built over the fortress next to the Hanging Church. You reach the entrance through a garden with three flower-covered pergolas and a fountain. It is a most interesting place and is rather like going over a stately home. Indeed many of the treasures have come from Coptic mansions, including some charming fountain floor recesses and screens. It has recently been completely refurbished, the lovely handcarved wooden ceilings and 'mushrabia' repaired and polished. Mushrabia is fine fretted woodwork cut in various geometrical designs. Made up without the use of nails or glue, it is delicately cut to fit together perfectly. Sometimes the interstices are filled with coloured glass. It is an art in which Egypt specializes and it is done today in exactly the same painstaking way as centuries ago. The great problem is keeping it free of dust, but long handled nylon brushes are used at the Coptic Museum. The exhibits are carefully labelled in English, French and Arabic and of course there is a catalogue with more details. A number of columns are displayed with capitals as unusual and varied as basketry design, rams' heads, inverted pyramids and acanthus leaves blowing in the breeze.

Leaving the Coptic Museum and all the other building over the old fortress, you can walk northwards a few hundred yards along Mari Girgis Street and you will come to the first mosque to be built by the Arabs in Egypt in the city of Fustat where they originally settled. The word fustat is probably a derivation from the Arabic word for camp. A story goes that when Babylon was besieged, the Arab commander, Amr Ibn el 'As, after whom the mosque was named, was elated because, as soon as his tent was pitched, a dove settled on top and immediately laid an egg. Amr commanded that the dove should not be moved. 'She has taken refuge under our protection. Leave the tent where it is until she has her brood and has flown away.' When the Romans were defeated, the city of Fustat grew up around the mosque. Another quotation attributed to Amr when he was first asked to describe Egypt, runs like this: 'Egypt is a dusty place and a green tree. Its length is a month, its breadth ten days. At one time Egypt is a white pearl, then golden amber, then a green emerald, then an embroidery of many colours.'

The burning of Fustat (1168 A.D.) was prompted by fear of invasion by the Crusaders. This damaged the mosque of Amr considerably and it has deteriorated and been restored countless times since then. It has always been famous for its 249 columns, no two alike. Many of these were collected together when it was first being built. It is believed that several Corinthian ones were brought from Heliopolis when that city was destroyed. Columns continued to be collected from other ruined buildings and, as in the Kairouan mosque in Tunisia and other mosques in Lebanon, somehow the result is pleasing. Not only do they vary in size, width and period but they are made of different kinds of stone such as granite, porphyry and ciproline. Much is being done today to restore famous buildings in Egypt and the mosque of Amr is to be one of them.

Leaving Fustat and its mosque, it is interesting to visit the nearby Nilometer on Roda Island. Built in 861 A.D. it is one of the historic monuments of Cairo. It consists of an octagonal column fixed in the centre of a deep well 19 feet (6 m) square. There is a depth scale in cubits reading up to 19 on it. The well is connected to the river and thus acted as a depth gauge. The walls and arches are decorated with kufic quotations. In ancient times the amount of tax levied was related to this depth scale. Such a simple device would not work nowadays since the level of the river is artificially controlled by the High Dam at Aswan.

The Citadel and nearby Mosques

Saladin's famous citadel, built in 1176, is one of Cairo's best known landmarks, made even more conspicuous by the slender minarets of the nearby mosques. At the end of Citadel Street, the two minarets of the mosque of Hassan can easily be seen, one being the loftiest in the city soaring some 300 feet (90 m). The mosque is considered by Islamic experts, to be the most beautiful in the Middle East. It is an enormous building covering some 9568 sq. yards

(8000 sq. m). The main entrance reaches upward with the grace of a gothic arch, decorated with stone tracery and topped by a shell design. It was built as a *medrasa*, a religious school, and had its own library, teachers and doctors. About 300 students lived in chambers above the prayer hall. The walls are three feet or a metre thick and the building was used as a fortress in times of trouble as can be seen on the outside walls where cannon balls have left their mark.

A battallion of Napoleon's soldiers sought refuge there during the Cairo rising of 1789 and looted much of its treasure, taking it off to their ships which Nelson was later to sink off Aboukir. Today, a team of French divers plan to try and retrieve one or two of these ships. It would be ironic of they were able to restore the treasure to the mosque. Within the building there is an open crenellated courtyard with a magnificent ablution fountain. It has marble panels surrounding it and overhead a dome is decorated with inscriptions from the Koran. Benches on which the faithful sit to wash are placed around it and are divided by slender columns studded with pieces of coloured marble. Beyond the courtyard, hanging from the vaulting, are numerous chains from which enamelled glass lanterns used to be suspended. You can see several of them in the Islamic Museum.

Most tombs in mosques are empty and the dead are buried in vaults below. Hassan's tomb does not contain the body of the founder, for it vanished mysteriously. The vault contains that of his son. The richly engraved minbar or pulpit is the largest in Egypt and it is said that, if you walk around it three times, you may have your wish granted. A nearby bronze door is damascened with gold and silver–but you have to get close to it to admire it, as dust is the enemy of large open buildings in Cairo. Because of this, the great inside walls have to be polished from top to bottom every ten years.

Across the street from the mosque of Hassan is the modern one of El Rifai, finished just before the first world war. Built by the Khedive Abbas Pasha, its raison d'être was to act as a mausoleum for the descendants of Muhammad Ali. Actually, only King Fuad (1868–1936) and King Farouk (1920–1965) are buried there. Recently, the late Shah of Iran was entombed there. It is a quiet beautiful building with a minbar (or pulpit) inlaid with ebony and mother of pearl and its carpets are exquisite in design and colour. The sun filters through high stained glass windows, relieving the sombre atmosphere.

It is but a short distance from these two mosques, to walk up the hill towards the Citadel which dominates the surrounding district on its spur jutting out from the Mokattem Hills. When you walk through the long archway into the Crusader–like castle, you realize how impregnable it must have been. No one could have known that better than the Mamelukes.

They came to Egypt from Turkey. They were originally foreign slaves and mercenaries captured during inter–tribal warfare. Eventually they became so powerful in Turkey that they were able to choose their own sultan and pursue their conquests abroad and that included Egypt. Despotic they may have been

Cairo minarets

but Cairo owes many of its most beautiful mosques to them. Later the Turks regained control of them but in Egypt, under Muhammad Ali, this only applied to Cairo and not the provinces. He was equally ruthless and, when the fellaheen tried to resist his conscription laws by putting out one eye of their male offspring, he promptly formed a one-eyed labour corps. The Mameluke era was finally ended by Napoleon at the Battle of the Pyramids in 1798.

During his reign, Muhammad Ali realized that the Mamelukes were plotting against him and invited them to come to Cairo to attend a lavish banquet in the Citadel. They arrived in their splendid robes on Arab steeds and raced through the great entrance of the Citadel. The gates slammed behind them and they were all massacred. Helpless before such treachery, only one Bey is said to have escaped. He galloped his charger to a low section of the wall and jumped over it. His name was Emin Bey, but whether he really jumped from that great height is not known. Perhaps he did not even attend the function. Whatever the truth, there are several paintings of him on horseback, literally jumping for his life and showing how this famous exploit may have been achieved.

Within the Citadel walls, the Muhammad Ali mosque is probably visited more by tourists than any other mosque in the city. People either love it or think it ostentatious. Built in 1829, it was designed by a Greek architect Yussef Boshna from Istanbul and the outside is a lovely replica of the famous Blue mosque there. Inside, the honey-coloured walls are said to be alabaster, taken from the cladding of one of the lesser pyramids of Giza. Sometimes it is called the Alabaster mosque. As you go in you can see on the right, Muhammad Ali's tomb.

The interior is so exquisitely carpeted that you are required to put on overshoes before entering. Although the great expanse within is empty save for the tomb, flanked by huge silver candlesticks and two minbars (one given by the late King Farouk) it hardly seems so because of the ornate decoration. Overhead, the dome and four smaller domes which surround it, are covered with mosaic, and rimmed around the whole are stained glass windows. Encircling rows of Islamic lamps and chandeliers are suspended from the ceiling, which highlight the carpeting below.

Outside in the courtyard, an intriguing object stands on a small tower. Known as the gingerbread clock, it was given to Muhammad Ali by King Louis Phillipe of France in 1815. In return, the King was sent the obelisk which now stands in the Place de la Concorde in Paris, where once was erected the infamous guillotine of the French Revolution.

To the south of the mosque, Muhammad Ali built a small palace which is now a museum. Two lions stand guard at the entrance and you can see some of the original furniture and in one corner, a wax figure of Muhammad Ali smoking his hookah. Cases are full of silver, china and objets d'art but the most interesting exhibit is a length of black brocade, hung on one wall with inscriptions from the Koran in silver. It is a length from a *Kiswa* or Holy

Carpet, which used to be sent to Mecca annually for the pilgrimage. The Kiswa started at the Citadel and was taken in parade through the streets of Cairo, before making its slow progress to Mecca, where it was placed on the great black stone called the *Kaabeh* during the festival and then cut up into pieces and presented to dignataries. As soon as one Kiswa left Cairo, the people who did the beautiful embroidery, started on the one for the following year. The practice was stopped only a few years ago. Nowadays, people travel by air.

It is rewarding to look out over the walls of the Citadel before you leave its precincts, because you will get an excellent view over the city. In the distance, you can even glimpse the ruins of the old aqueduct which at one time supplied the water from the Nile. Even further away, on a clear day, the Pyramids of Giza can be seen. Minarets of different designs, but all topped with graceful half moons–the sign of Islam–are numerous. There is a saying that if a Muslim went to a different mosque every day of the year, he could not enter all those in Cairo. The City of the Dead, with its domes huddled close together, is easily discerned. Closer to the onlooker are the mosques of Hassan, El Rifai and Ibn Tulun–the oldest in the city–and the Gayer Anderson museum. The two latter almost seem to touch the ramparts and are easy to visit before you leave the district.

Ahmed Ibn Tulun, son of Mameluke and founder of the Tulunid dynasty, built his mosque in 878 A.D. A rectangular stone edifice, it is in sharp contrast to that of Muhammad Ali. Although simple inside, it has 129 windows of different shapes and decoration. The mihrab, indicating the direction of Mecca for prayers, is inset with coloured marble and gilded mosaics; this and the hand-carved wooden pulpit are attributed to Sultan Lagin el Mansur in 1296 A.D. The interior open courtyard is 300 feet (90 m) square. On three sides it is surrounded by cloisters consisting of two rows of columns. In the shadow, the tracery of the window grilles rests against the blue of the sky and there is an atmosphere of serenity as you walk along the cool colonnades between the great piers. On the fourth side which faces Mecca, the aisles are five rows deep and in the centre of the court is the usual domed fountain.

The minaret rises beyond the walls of the mosque to the northwest. It is charmingly simple in style with a winding external staircase leading to the gallery above. A story has it that Ibn Tulun was toying one day with a piece of paper and, twisting it around in a spiral, ordered that it be copied for the minaret.

Of historic houses open to the public, the Gayer Anderson is probably the best known. During the seventeenth century, Sheik es Sinhaimi bought two antiquated houses standing cheek by jowl and joined them together by their top floors. The dwelling had direct access to the north east entrance of the Ibn Tulun mosque. About fifty years ago, an Englishman, Major Gayer Anderson, a great collector of Egyptian furniture and antiques of different periods, bought the house to restore it and contain his acquisitions. He lived there for

Ibn Tulun mosque. Its minaret is said to be the earliest in Cairo

many years and, being gregarious, entertained a great deal. When he died in 1942 he bequeathed the house and contents to the Egyptian Government.

The house is attractive, even on the outside, where there are overhanging mushrabia balconies and shutters. On the top floor, an ornate cupboard conceals a hidden doorway which probably led into the harem quarters long ago. Mushrabia screens still give the view that the ladies enjoyed of the large reception hall on the ground floor with a sunken mosaic fountain in the centre. The house is completely furnished, though in a haphazard way. There are several paintings and gilded ikons and a statue of the Cat God, Bast. One interesting drawing of Gayer Anderson himself, shows his features superimposed on the Sphinx.

'Mushrabia' balconies

Many visitors have their own favourite mosque, more often than not one that they have inspected casually so it is always worthwhile if you have a little time to spare to explore one on your own. The Victorian writer, Robert Hichens, loved one he called the Blue mosque because of its beautiful delphinium blue tiles. Guides sometimes ask if you would like them to call out the name of Allah in a mosque. If you agree, they will do so in ringing tones which can produce amazing echoes.

Islamic Museum

Visitors interested in Islamic art should not miss seeing the Islamic Museum. Not only is it unique in the world but many of the exhibits are irreplaceable. It was the far-seeing Khedive Ismail who thought of building such a museum to preserve some of the nation's treasures, but his idea did not come to fruition during his lifetime or that of his son Tawfik. Precious objects were brought from mosques and monuments and stored in the mosque of El Hakim until finally in 1903, they were put on display in the present museum in Bab el Khalq Square which was shared with the National Library. Only recently has the latter been moved to another building and the additional space is proving invaluable. Months of restoration, cleaning, painting and sorting has gone on and it has greatly improved the museum. The newly opened coin room has an amazing collection of gold coins displayed in glass cases, one of the oldest being an Islamic dinar, struck by an Omayyad Caliph in the first year of Hijrah (726 A.D.).

In the Koran collection, the oldest parchment dates back to the eighth century. The earliest tombstone with kufic writing comes from the Nile valley and is dated 31 A.D. There are sixty Mameluke glass lamps and some lustra painted ceramics from the Fatimid period. Egyptian potters were the first to perfect the 'lustre' painting technique. There are interesting wooden panels from the Western Fatimid Palace at Fustat, which show scenes from court life including hunting and listening to musicians. More finds from Fustat include fresco painting and carpet fragments.

Room 20 is hung with marvellous carpets, many being prayer rugs. One under glass, of black brocade with silver threads, is a length from yet another Kiswa. There is a room of beautiful tiles and another of military weapons such as swords, armour, chain mail and even a cannon used at the Battle of the Pyramids. A section is given over to navigation with astrolabes. Another hall has rooms of different periods set up, tiled and furnished.

Al Azhar Mosque and University

Begun in 972 A.D., a few months after the Fatimid conquest of Egypt, this enormous mosque and university stands facing the street and in the district of the same name. Al Azhar means 'The Splendid' and the university is the oldest in existence and considered to be the greatest Islamic place of learning. Students come from all over the Middle and Far East. Its library alone contains over 80,000 volumes and manuscripts. Al Azhar, with its minarets and domes, is the centrepiece of this old part of the city known as Fatimid Cairo. The rector and his staff wear the same type of robe that tutors have worn there for a thousand years, dark blue galabiehs of fine wool and white turbans. The original rectangular form of the building remains, although after an earthquake in 1903 the mosque had to be rebuilt. Frequent restorations and additions have been made, though the character of the building has been preserved. Charity has always been a part of Al Azhar's tradition; the blind were cared for and even up to a century ago it was estimated that no less than forty thousand individuals would call every alternate day when bread and oil for lamps would be distributed.

The first mosques had no minarets. It was not until Amr's mosque at Fustat was built that the first minaret was designed, inspired by the Pharos, the great lighthouse in Alexandria, one of the seven wonders of the ancient world. The Arabic word for lighthouse is 'Minar'. One of the chambers at the top of the Pharos was a place of worship–closer to the gods, it was believed, than if built on the ground. Minarets are of different designs and sizes which is part of their charm. Usually they are square from the ground to the top of the mosque walls, then octagonal above. The upper portion is divided into two or three parts, the top section being set back to make room for the balcony, from which the call to prayer is sung by the 'muezzin'. The call begins with the words 'Allah is Great and Muhammad is his prophet'. Tape recordings are sometimes used today. Nevertheless the sung prayer is dignified and appealing, particularly at sunset, and serves to remind the Muslim of his God. Al Azhar has no less than five minarets, each different and one with a twin dome on top.

The university part of Al Azhar appears bigger than it is because, although much of it is covered in, more of it is open to the sky. High columned cloisters seem like long avenues in a forest. Hundreds of students in small groups have their places reserved under niches and porticoes where they gather round their tutors. Beautiful hand woven rugs and carpets are strewn over the stone flooring, red being the dominant colour. The students go barefoot on them and visitors must wear cloth slippers over their shoes. As you wander around this magnificent building admiring the delicate stone tracery, mosaic and kufic characters, you wonder how so many beautiful geometrical designs are possible. Mosque decoration must have no human, animal or plant figures, in case they should detract from prayer and contemplation.

There are eight entrances. The Door of the Barbers, so called because students had to be clean shaven, is in the western facade and leads to the magnificent central open courtyard. Above the crenellated edges of the walls you can see the arabesque details of the minarets. As tourists cannot visit during teaching or prayer periods, it is difficult for them to visualize that space is at a premium. For instance during lecture hours one small roofed chamber has four corners with students from different countries in each.

Khan El Khalili and the Muski

The two adjoining bazaar areas, the Khan el Khalili and the Muski, are often confused by Egyptians and foreigners alike. They lie astride the Muski street which runs from Ataba Square to Sayedna el Hussein Square. The Khan el Khalili is the larger bazaar. The original khan or caravanserai was built in 1382 by Amir Garkas el Khalili, hence the name.

You can start your walk from the gate of Bab Zuweila, a gate that once gave access to the old walled city of Cairo. The street, humming with life, is lined with shops offering the necessities of Egyptian life, from harnesses for donkeys and camels to travelling ovens for baking sweet potatoes, little lamps for Ramadan, bird cages and son on. Eventually you come to Bab Zuweila. Opposite its porch is the Khiyameya, once a covered market where tents of coarse canvas are now made. These tents are in common use and are planted in the middle of a street at weddings and funerals, to serve as a reception room. On the unbleached canvas, brightly coloured fabrics are laid to form traditional arabesques. To please tourists, the craftsmen also make some amusing stitched patchwork scenes, images of the Pharaonic era such as the

A corner of the Khan el Khalili bazaar in Cairo

'weighing of the heart' or Ramses in his chariot drawing a bow. You will also find more modern designs like a stubborn little donkey, a patient fisherman or a belly dancer.

Seven hundred metres away is the main Khan el Khalili, still the favourite haunt of visitors and Egyptians alike. This souk, founded on the site once occupied by the tombs of the Fatimid Caliphs, is crammed with rows and layers of shops full of attractive articles. Here you will encounter the typical and all-pervasive aroma of tobacco, attar, fish and perfume. You can look at the shops selling carpets, curtains and cloth. You can watch the wood carver and artists in mother-of-pearl and ivory. Further the jewellers and goldsmiths offer their products: just nearby are shops for leather goods and engraved articles, where you can see silver thread painstakingly worked into copper and brass. Do not hesitate to look round or accept the tea or coffee which you may be offered. This is but the expression of Egyptian hospitality. Even if you do not buy anything, they are pleased to have had the chance of chatting with you. If you have your eye on something, then haggle over the price without any embarrassment and you will raise their estimation of you as you lower the prices. It is best to look around the shops before buying to ensure that you buy what you really want—or get something you can watch being made and explain exactly how you would like it.

The Egyptian perfumer is famed. He can blend a scent specially for you. Small phials of essences of flowers and other fragrances are held under your nose. You are assured that each is more exotic than the last until you make up your mind which you find most alluring.

The making of amber necklaces is fascinating to watch. Pieces of amber are turned into polished rounds on crude lathes, producing honey-coloured beads smooth to the touch. Muslims buy them as Roman Catholics buy rosaries to hold and slip through their fingers as they whisper the various names of Allah. Perhaps semi-precious stones appeal and there are countless others besides amber which you can buy made up or in an uncut state.

You will be shown zircons with their flashing blues, blue-greens or red-browns, opals with their rich varied tints, amethysts, tawny topazes, garnets and the brittle, colourful tourmalines. Of the real gems, emeralds seem to vary most in price. All are lovely, from the lustrous dark greens (which are the most costly) to the pale ones. When diamonds, rubies and sapphires were unknown, emeralds were highly prized in ancient Egypt. Among jewels in the tombs of the Princesses Ita and Khumit, embalmed 4000 years ago, a bronze dagger was found, studded with emeralds and, amongst the jewelry made of the usual cornelian and lapis lazuli, was a necklace with a clasp of emeralds and a strand of emerald beads.

The silver filigree work is cheap but very pretty. The tracery patterns look fragile but are deceptively strong. Filigree castings of silver and gold enfold charming little scent bottles with jewelled tops. If you are hesitant about buying, the merchants understand, and you can always return another day if you wish.

Leaving the Khan el Khalili and returning to central Cairo you pass along streets with many shops, boutiques and restaurants. Shopping is irresistible for tourists and, close to the Nile Corniche, near the famed Shepheards and the new Intercontinental hotels and facing the US Embassy, you will find Karnak Bazaar. It reaches back almost to the Corniche and is a fascinating emporium. Already one side has a facade decorated with Pharaonic carvings which, although the work of modern craftsmen, proves that they have lost none of the skills of their forebears. Within you will find Egyptian ornaments beautifully lit and displayed, ivory figures, antiques, translucent alabaster goblets, statues of gods and goddesses, brass and copper vases inlaid with silver. There are engraved Islamic lamps, plates, gold and silver jewelry sparkling with gems and priceless rugs. This modern Aladdin's cave is owned by Morsi el Gabry.

Morsi has designed many gifts for heads of state and, when the Camp David meetings ended, he had three identical trays made for Presidents Carter and Sadat and Premier Begin. They were circular, with carvings of the Christian cross, the Islamic crescent and the Star of David intermingled in the centre.

Around the edges were depicted scenes from the life of Moses and episodes common to the Bible, the Koran and the Torah.

Morsi makes every minute of his day count and never seems to tire, probably because he always enjoys what he is doing. He greets visitors to his bazaar enthusiastically over the inevitable cup of Turkish coffee and you can arrange a party in his Arab tent close to the pyramids. To wander through the shop is to enter a half-dream world, part museum and part bazaar and, if you have not the time or the inclination to visit the Muski, you will find almost as great a variety here. One tourist, told to go and buy things at Karnak, remarked 'Don't tell me Morsi owns that temple in Luxor!'

As you leave Karnak Bazaar and walk along the Nile Corniche towards Roda Island, you will see Air France's Meridien Hotel which is on the tip of the island. From its dining room you can imagine you are sailing on the Nile.

Manial Palace

About the centre of Roda Island and reached by another bridge is Manial Palace, part of which is now a museum. One of King Farouk's family, Prince Muhammad Ali, was fond of the Roda formal gardens and parkland (which had been the site of the palace of the Baharite Mamelukes) and acquired some 15 acres (6 hectares) sixty years ago. Over a period of forty years he had the present palace built exactly to suit his taste. He was passionately fond of horses and you will find the horse motif everywhere, from paintings of his Arab steeds to the saddle-like chairs around the table in the dining room. The palace consists of several buildings full of hand made furniture, antiques, jewelry, costumes, alabaster fountains, golden goblets and even, it is said, a tuft of the prophet's beard in a carved chest which was given to the Prince by his mother who had received it as a present from a Turkish Sultan.

The most magnificent room is the golden hall with palm shaped gilded columns and magnificent crystal chandeliers. The innumerable slender pillars, inlaid walls, floors and strangely beautiful stalactite ceilings, wrought in the same style as the Alhambra in Granada, make more than one visit essential. The garden has several, centuries-old banyan trees, palm trees from the West Indies, different types of cacti and many exotic flowers.

Northward along the Nile from Roda Island and across the Tahrir Bridge, there is Gezira Island, with the El Borg hotel and the Andalusian Gardens full of unusual trees and flowers. The new Gezira Sheraton hotel, has been built on the southern tip of the island and so is only a short distance from the older Cairo Sheraton on the west bank. Both have marinas on the Nile. The Gezira Sheraton is a 27 floor circular tower, commanding magnificent views in all directions. A short distance away in mid-Nile is the Geneva-style fountain, currently out of action but hopefully to be restored. The top eight floors offer exclusive suites with their own reception desk and lift–a hotel within a hotel. It is rumoured that, having erected a crane to assist with the building, the

One of the halls on display at Manial Palace

contractors had not considered the problem of removing it when the tower had been built round it. It was eventually removed in small pieces.

The famous Gezira Sporting Club is in the centre of the island, with its delightful club house, golf course, swimming pool, squash courts, lawns and flower beds. Unfortunately, its amenities no longer include the serving of alcohol.

The Cairo Tower on the island is still the tallest concrete building in the country and from the top, as has been said before, you can get a view of the whole of Cairo. There are telescopes in the viewing gallery but whether you use them or not, the views are equally impressive. To the far west, the lush greenery, sliced into tiny squares by blue irrigation canals ends abruptly in bone dry sand. Bunched in the desert lie the three great tawny pyramids of Giza. Beyond them you can see the Step Pyramid at Sakkara. Far away, another line of pyramids look like regimented toys against the horizon. Closer to hand, there is the modern section of Cairo and the faculty buildings of Cairo University. Eastward is the commercial centre with its high blocks of new flats, shops and banks, divided by tree-lined streets.

Gezira is the largest Nile island in Cairo and Zamalek, a pleasant residential area with parkland and trees edging down to the river, is part of it. Gezira Palace was built by the Khedive Ismail for the Empress Eugenie and other royal guests at the opening of the Suez Canal festivities in 1869. Surrounded by gardens and fountains, the Khedive commanded that the appartments for the Empress should be replicas of those she occupied in the Tuilleries in Paris so that, during her visit, she would feel at home. The palace is now part of the Marriott Hotel. The original palace is flanked by two tower blocks of bedrooms and the palace interior has been renovated, regilded and decorated. The great stairways have new carpets, glistening chandeliers hang from the ceilings and the Aida ballroom, covering some 8000 square feet (743 sq.m) can accomodate 1300 guests for a reception. Part of the formal gardens have made way for tennis courts, swimming pool and separate health clubs for men and women.

Leaving Gezira Island and turning south into Giza Street along the west bank of the Nile, you pass by Cairo's Zoological Gardens on your right. They cover some 50 acres (20 hectares) and there are about 600 animals. It was there that I saw my first black panther, a beautiful creature with fur gleaming like black satin and eyes of vivid amber. The zoo is open from 8.30 in the morning until sunset. It is an attractive place for a walk beneath flowering trees and many of the paths are of patterned mosaic.

Next to the zoological gardens is Cairo University, one of the largest in the Middle East and well-known for its medical and engineering facilities. Amongst its library treasures are some original paintings by artists who were part of Napoleon's entourage when his army invaded Egypt. The university was founded by King Fuad who had a royal suite there which is now used for V.I.P.s. It is the epitome of luxury complete with a black marble bathroom. The campus clock is a small replica of London's Big Ben.

Papyrus Institute

A short distance south from the Cairo Sheraton along the Nile bank is the Papyrus Institute of Doctor Hassan Ragab. It has its gallery and offices in a houseboat. He set it up more than a decade ago. For some years he had studied the growth of the papyrus plant and the way it was made into sheets and used by the Pharaonic scribes. He started to cultivate the plant on the river bank and revived the whole production process as it was originally done. Artists were employed to do paintings on it and the result caught on with visitors as it is readily portable and very attractive. Of course in the intervening years there have been many imitations, some good and some not so good, but a visit to the original establishment is well worth your time. In the back of the doctor's mind was another idea which he has brought to fruition. Jacob's Island in the Nile had been used by him for papyrus growing. Why not create a Pharaonic village there and bring the past back to life as he had done with the papyrus fabrication?

Ibis headed Thoth, God of scribes and writing, seen from the theatre barge at Dr Ragab's island in Cairo

Isis suckling Horus seen from the theatre barge at Dr Ragab's island in Cairo

Papyrus boat building on Dr Ragab's island in Cairo

Pharaonic Village

You board a barge with rising tiers of seats facing to one side and this is towed slowly along canals in the island. Thus the audience is brought to the scenes rather than the usual theatre system. This enables the presentation of a succession of *tableaux vivants* depicting most of the usual occupations of ancient Egypt. Corn is threshed, papyrus boats are being built, there is bee keeping in mud hives and tilling of the earth using wooden tools. You pass replica statues of the gods and both commentator and barge pause frequently for photography. For six months, some 500 people were trained to make these scenes realistic. You go ashore at one point and enter a typical house to see exactly how people lived and the whole presentation is delightfully unusual.

There is a temple with a mummification chamber and, at the other extreme, a poor man's house. Animals make up part of the farming scenes. The costumes are not only authentic but are made of linen, as cotton was not discovered until centuries later. To blot out nearby buildings and chimneys, 5000 trees were planted round the island, and this enhances the effect of transition into the past.

Madame Sadat

Before continuing along the Giza road to the outskirts of Cairo, you pass the late President Sadat's house, where his wife Jehan still lives. My husband Tony and I had been invited to see her one morning. Sadek, the excellent driver we sometimes have in Cairo, drove quickly but skilfully through a guarded

Pharaonic living tableau on Dr Ragab's island in Cairo

gateway; then between lawns edged with trees, catching glimpses of peacocks spreading vividly coloured tails against the green. We came to a halt by a flight of marble steps and a young black labrador bounded forward to greet us. We were shown through a spacious hallway into a drawing room. A *safragi* or servant offered mango juice in crystal glasses, which we sipped while awaiting the arrival of Madame Sadat. Behind the sofa where I sat, hung a Gobelin tapestry depicting a hunting scene with hounds leaping through a forest. The walls were cream, the furniture upholstered in ivory and gold brocade. Egyptian rugs of geometrical design were strewn on the parquet floor. It was a quiet room and from the picture windows we watched the Nile flow sluggishly by beyond a helicopter pad.

Suddenly, tapping footsteps announced our hostess. 'You are early', she said, 'I hope I have not kept you waiting. I have just returned from lecturing at the university.' I admitted we were early and assured her that this particular morning, the traffic had seemed to melt before us. 'That is a miracle that may never happen again', she laughed.

Jehan Sadat has an Anglo-Egyptian background. Her Egyptian father worked in the Ministry of Health in Cairo; her English mother, formerly Gladys Cottrell, came from Sheffield. Before thinking of going to university, she married Anwar Sadat at the age of seventeen. They had three daughters and one son. 'Not only was I their mother' she says, 'I was also their nanny.' Yet as they grew up and attended school, in the back of her mind was the question 'Why not continue my studies?' It was, she says 'a kind of challenge'. Her husband suggested history or geography, but she chose literature and has never regretted it.

Her degree thesis was on the influence of Shelley on Arabic literature. Today she is a part-time lecturer at Cairo University. Her ability to teach, head committees, and at the same time see members of her family has often been remarked upon but, as she says with a smile, 'My life has not been what you call usual.'

Attractive, socially adept and intellectually bright, Jehan entered her role as First Lady of Egypt when Anwar Sadat became President. Unlike other leaders wives in the Arab world, she accompanied her husband on various official visits and missions. She took television and radio interviews in her stride, spoke at women's clubs and received degrees at several international universities. She readily understood that her husband's idea of coexistence between Arab and Jew would solve many Middle Eastern problems. Sadat's olive-branch mission to Jerusalem, which paved the way to the Camp David discussions in America, gave every indication of success. Fate decreed otherwise and all too soon came Sadat's brutal assassination. It was the bitterest blow Jehan had received. Heartbroken, she clung to the desire to further her husband's ideals.

Several months later, in Britain, she spoke at the Woman of the Year luncheon, which was televised. She made an eloquent plea for world peace. Her appearance on this occasion made an unforgettable impression. She was still in mourning and wore a simple black dress without jewellery. Her fair hair, as always, was beautifully styled. Her face was thinner which made her brown eyes larger and more appealing. There was a short silence when she finished and then thunderous applause.

As the clapping continued, I was reminded of happier times in the seventies, when I was first presented to her after she opened a bazaar at the old Semiramis hotel facing the Nile. She had made a short speech and then went to visit the various stalls. A smartly dressed lady at one of them bent forward to me and whispered 'How beautiful she is. Just what one imagines a President's wife should be'.

Jehan broke into my thoughts by asking 'Would you like to see the river from the sitting room upstairs?' As we followed her, Tony enquired about the labrador which had greeted us at the threshold. 'His name is Duke and he is a gift from American friends,' she replied. 'He is always the first to welcome me when I come home. I love animals and plants.' 'I can see that,' I laughed, as I bent under a palm tree growing in a Chinese container. I stopped at its base not only to see the exquisite workmanship, but to admire the half-life-size silver deer near it. Jehan stroked its antlers and I asked if she would pose by it for a photograph. 'Willingly' she said. 'He is peaceful but on the alert like Anubis in your Antiquities Museum' I said. 'Have you ever been to Denmark and visited the Rosenborg Palace in Copenhagen?' 'No' said Jehan. I explained how, in the palace, which is open to the public, there are three similar, almost life-size lions made in silver with golden manes, which stand guard before an ivory throne in the banqueting hall. Somewhat whimsical, they pose in playful attitudes. One seems about to jump into the air with its front legs flat on the floor, another is looking towards the throne, while the third is sitting down but on the alert, just in case there might be any danger. These engaging animals have guarded the throne since 1665 and, when Danish kings die, are placed round the coffin during the lying-in-state.

As Jehan led us through various rooms, we saw more ornamental animals, including life-size silver ducks and a tiny Lalique elephant. Plants were everywhere. The dining room was small and intimate. Paintings of Cairo street scenes hung on the walls of the sitting room whose windows overlooked the Nile. 'The river reminds me of my childhood,' said Jehan. 'I grew up on Roda Island where my parents had a house. Before Anwar became President and when we had more time, if he wished to take me for an evening drive, he always knew where I wanted to go–Roda Island to watch the sunset. Perhaps sunsets are one of the reasons that rose is my favourite colour. Another pastime we loved was fishing in the river.' 'Which temple along the Nile do you like best?' I asked. 'They are all like my children,' she replied. 'You love each one for different reasons.' She reflected a moment. 'You know, I often think of the countries in the Middle East which have abundant oil and then it strikes me that perhaps we are the most fortunate. We have this blessing, this great waterway, the Nile.'

3

THE PYRAMIDS OF

GIZA

AND

ENVIRONS

OF

CAIRO

Since the days of the Grand tour, the prime reason for visiting Egypt has always been to see the Pyramids and Sphinx at Giza. One wonders which would be chosen first if they were not so close together. As son-et-lumière has added immeasurably to their fascination, they are now more popular than ever before. Nightly performances are in different languages, so be sure you go when it is in English.

Giza is some 7 miles (10 km) from the centre of Cairo and you follow the Giza Road which leads into the Pyramids Road. The original road was specifically constructed by Khedive Ismail, so that the Empress Eugenie could be driven from her palace along the Nile to see the Pyramids. A chalet was built at their base to house her and her suite for a single night. She thought the monuments were magnificent and was delighted as darkness fell that, instead of fireworks, magnesium flares were used to illuminate them.

Today, the Pyramids Road is lined on either side with hotels. villas, blocks of flats and night clubs. Down the centre of the road, the tram tracks have been replaced by attractive topiary. Because it is so built up you may be surprised by the sudden appearance of the Great Pyramid against the skyline. It is impossible to convey the immensity of it. Men have tried for centuries and the only answer is to see it for oneself. To describe it as the most gigantic piece of architecture in the world does not help, nor does Napoleon's famous battle cry when his army was assembled near the plain of Giza. 'Soldiers, forty centuries look down upon you.' The great general was not a learned archaeologist, for Cheops Pyramid was ancient when Abraham first went to live in Egypt. What a magnificent sight it must have been then, complete with its outer casing gleaming in the distance like the sun itself. It is the only one of the seven wonders of the ancient world that is left for us to admire and it is the greatest.

Herodotus, that father of history, says that one hundred thousand workmen–changing every three months for ten years–were employed in making a causeway for the conveyance of stones, and that twenty years more

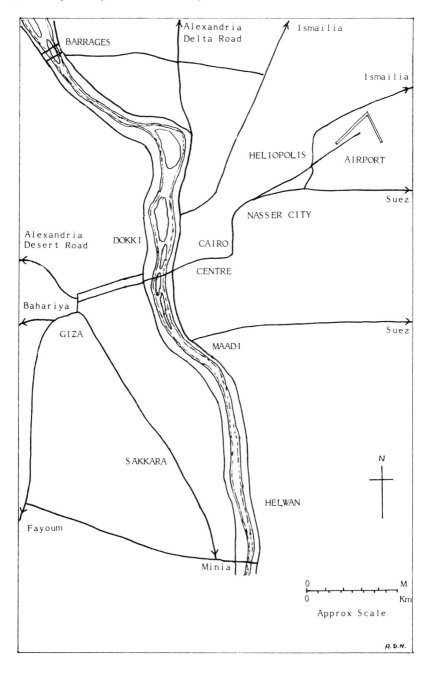

were spent in building the Great Pyramid itself. The historian also records that 1600 talents of silver were spent in buying radishes, onions and garlic for the labourers!

Inside the pyramid there are a series of corridors and rooms which are not recommended for anyone who suffers from claustrophobia. They were made to deceive those who tried to steal the trappings and treasures of the Pharaoh. All visitors enter Cheops Pyramid by way of a tunnel cut out horizontally from the north face called 'Mamun's Hole' after Khalif al Ma'mun who opened the pyramid from this side in 820 A.D. This narrow corridor joins another about 300 feet (90 m) long, then one climbs a little and finally reaches the main burial chamber. There are no decorations or inscriptions and the treasures vanished long ago. The interior is in no way as rewarding as the tombs in the Valley of the Kings.

The second pyramid, that of Chephren, is slightly smaller than that of his father but, being set up further on the Giza plateau, appears to be as high if not higher. Pieces of the original cladding still adhere to the summit and it looks equally magnificent in sunlight or when the moon is full. The third pyramid is that of Mycerinus, Cheops' grandson, who was the fifth king of the Fourth Dynasty. It is 218 (66 m) feet high and the smallest of the three. Its base is still encased in unfinished granite blocks.

The gargantuan triangles of the pyramids have acted as background for many unusual performances as dissimilar as the opera *Aida* and the Old Vic Company, but nothing is as moving as when a spectral voice comes over the sands and begins the son-et-lumière commentary. 'You have come tonight to the most fabulous and celebrated place in the world. Here on the plateau of Giza stands forever the mightiest of human achievements. No traveller, Emperor, merchant or poet has trodden on these sands and not gasped in awe.'

You can now leave Heathrow in the morning on Concorde, be served a champagne breakfast en route, have a day's sightseeing in Cairo, including a visit to the Pyramids and Sphinx, lunch at the Mena House Oberoi Hotel and be back in London that evening. Very expensive but very exciting. It would be interesting to know what Cheops would have made of it if 5000 years ago he had seen a heavenly pyramidal shape hurtle over his earthly one in a split second. Perhaps a shooting star?

The Sphinx is close to the Chephren Pyramid. During the reign of Cheops, her body lay hidden, blanketed by desert sand, but her head gazed out over the Nile with its famed inscrutibility. The enormous statue was so called by Herodotus from the Greek name for a compound creature with human head and lion's body and has been known as the Sphinx ever since. It is fairly certain that it was created during the rule of the Pharaohs of the Old Kingdom. To the ancient Egyptians the ancient figure was a colossal image of the God of the Rising Sun, conqueror of darkness; the God of the Morning–Harmachis. Between the great paws lies a tablet. It records that Harmachis appeared to Thothmes IV when he was in a deep sleep and promised to present the crown

The Sphinx and the Chephren Pyramid at Giza

of Egypt to him on one condition. The God's own body must first be released from the sand that had accumulated over it for centuries. This was done and Harmachis was fully revealed to Man once more. The great lion's body is 150 feet (46 m) long, the front legs stretching out a further 50 feet (15 m). The head rises 70 feet (21 m) into the air, a long lion's tail curved up over the haunches.

Cheops and his son Chephren probably repaired the mysterious stone god some two thousand seven-hundred years before Christ. The age of the Sphinx is unknown. Like any international beauty, she guards that secret well. No historian has been prepared to say when she did *not* exist. At her paws sacrifices were offered. Ramses the Great was among her worshippers and inscriptions on her paws testify that later the Romans did likewise. Men from every country have painted her. She has been photographed more than any other monument in the world. Silently she sits, looking to the east, waiting for the dawn of a new day.

Traditional ways to visit the pyramids

For those who have not already visited the Giza plateau, the son-et-lumière display is perhaps the most fascinating way to begin acquaintance with the great monuments. If you can follow this with a second visit at sunset when most of the tourists have gone, it is a most rewarding experience. The setting sun each evening strikes them with glowing colours and the sand underfoot is still warm from the day.

The traditional way to see the Pyramids is by riding a camel. Your bus will stop at a caravanserai about a quarter of a mile away, where those who wish can disembark and go on by camel, horse or pony and trap. The bus carries on to the Pyramids and waits for the sightseers to return to it. The camel boys deck their steeds with colourful wool tassles hung from bridle and saddle. Camel saddles are often inlaid with mother-of-pearl and ivory and tourists can buy them as souvenirs.

You must not leave the plateau until you have seen the most beautiful object there, Cheops' Solar Boat, housed in its own air-conditioned building in

The Solar Boat in its air-conditioned museum next to the Great Pyramid

the shadow of the Great Pyramid. It is 4000 years older than the Viking ships in Scandinavia and was built centuries before Moses brought the Ten Commandments down from Mount Sinai. Just as the Great Pyramid, weighing five million tons, was created to house Pharaoh Cheops' body, so this huge gondola was intended to carry his soul–his Ka–through the waters of the Underworld to eternal life.

Discovered in 1954, it is the greatest find since that of Tutankhamun's tomb by Carter in 1922. It is known as the Day Boat and there is almost certainly another one–the Night Boat–lying in a similar pit nearby. After the difficulties encountered by the Antiquities Department in guarding this one from deterioration once it was exposed to the air, it has been decided to postpone further excavation for a second boat and leave it cocooned in its naturally preservative grave for the moment. Indeed the present boat has only been adequately housed quite recently and is now slowly regaining the large amount of moisture which it lost from its timbers in its years above ground.

It has taken a long time to reassemble the boat–it was stored in its pit stripped down–and display it properly. As its museum is long and narrow, it is not possible to stand back and get an overall view of the boat. However, if you examine the excellent scale model near the entrance you will have a clear picture in your mind. About 150 feet (46 m) long, it resembles a giant Venetian gondola. Visitors have to put on special overboots to minimize dust in the chamber and are not permitted to take their cameras in with them. The planks are made of Lebanese cedar, some over 70 feet (21 m) long, many notched at the edges to enhance rigidity and all sewn together with hemp rope and wooden pegs. There were no other fastenings 6000 years ago and, assuming that the Underworld river is as wet as the Nile, the ropes and pegs would swell and ensure a watertight structure. The ornate bow and stern are in the form of bundles of papyrus reeds with flowering tops. On deck is a cabin with a double roof having a space between its layers into which fresh palm fronds were packed to keep the interior cool. Who said air-conditioning was new!

Propulsion was by ten oars, five each side, which, from the markings on them, were probably designed also to serve as weapons if necessary. Steering was accomplished by two even larger oars.

The story of the Solar Boat's discovery is scarcely less fascinating than the find itself. Through it a most gifted scholar and Egyptologist, Kamal el Mallakh, has become a legend in his own lifetime. When the Tutankhamun exhibition in London was opened by Queen Elizabeth II, Doctor Mukhtar, Director of the Egyptian Antiquities Museum, presented Kamal to her as the 'Carter of today'. Kamal bowed and gave a greeting in Pharaonic language. The Queen asked that it be translated and was charmed to learn that it was a phrase used to wish the Pharaoh blessing and longevity, whether male or female. It is significant that there was equality of the sexes in Pharaonic times—but then who could forget Cleopatra and Hatshepsut?

Close by the side of the Great Pyramid which overlooks the Sphinx, a road was being made for the convenience of tourists. Kamal was asked to keep an eye on the digging. His excitement was great when his men dug down to limestone powder–not the kind that capped Chephren's Pyramid, but of the type found in the Mokkatam Hills on the other side of Cairo. As the men continued to dig they came upon a pinkish cement which sealed together large slabs. These seemed to form a flat base or roof. Kamal was of the latter opinion but it was difficult to be sure and often important finds seem imminent, only to end in disappointment. Perhaps the slabs formed part of the foundation of Cheops' Pyramid. Kamal had been working on the Giza site for some years and it was the first time he felt that Cheops' Solar Boat might be uncovered. The area was in the exact position that would have been logically chosen. Boat pits by the lesser pyramid had yielded nothing and, even if there had been a boat, it might have been robbed in antiquity. He felt he would be satisfied if only some vestiges of a Solar Boat were found.

Together with the team of men he cleared an area large enough to see that the slabs might indeed be a roof. He then began to scrape down between two blocks which seemed less sturdy than the others. He cut a deep chink between

Kamal el Mallakh explains how he discovered the Solar Boat using a model. Visitors wear special overboots to minimize dust in the chamber

the two. On May 26, 1954 he began digging in earnest. He kept on until the hole was large enough for him to be lowered into it head first. He continued to cut and scrape.

As he became accustomed to the gloom, he was able to work more quickly and the casing soon began to crumble and give way. Time meant nothing and he was hardly aware of being suspended head downwards in cramped and dusty conditions. Suddenly his head went through into empty nothingness and an almost imperceptible smell assailed his nostrils. Then he recognized it as cedar wood and realized a sense of fulfilment he had never known before. He knew that there was more than a chance that the wood might have been pulverized by white ants, but he still dared to hope.

A mirror was passed down so that he could reflect the sunlight into the cavity. He brought his hand down gently and twisted into a new position to reach as far as possible into the aperture and reflect the light from behind him. The smell of cedar wood was now unmistakable and then, suddenly, the tip of an oar was struck by the sun. 'It is the boat', he shouted and willing hands pulled him upwards. His men were beside themselves with joy. 'Mabrouk, mabrouk', (congratulations) they cried, tears streaming down their faces.

Kamal held his hand to his forehead and felt something hot and sticky. He looked at his hand and found that it was covered with blood. He had jammed his head into the hole so hard that he had gashed himself without being aware of it or feeling any pain. He still has a white indentation in his forehead. 'I suppose it is an honourable scar', he says.

Sakkara and Memphis

From the Great Pyramid plateau you can se the Pyramid of Zoser at Sakkara about ten miles to the south, across the desert. Opposite the camel caravanserai where you stopped on your way up, is the famous Mena House Oberoi hotel. Largely surrounded by trees and ornamental gardens, the older part of it fades naturally into the pyramid scene.

The hotel was originally the Royal Lodge of Khedive Ismail who used it as a guest house for friends who wished to visit the Pyramids and Sphinx. As the years went by it changed hands many times and, like Midas, it always attracted wealth and was enlarged extensively until it became a luxury hotel. Antiques were brought from various towns in Egypt, including screens and furniture of 'mushrabia'. In the 1880s at a time when balconies and swimming pools were unheard of, each bedroom at Mena House had an open balcony leading from French windows, so that guests could enjoy having their breakfasts out of doors if they wished. The large swimming pool, believed to be the first one in any hotel, was of marble. In the days before efficient filtration plants existed it was emptied every night, scrubbed by a team of servants and refilled ready for the guests next morning. It has now been replaced by a large modern one in which you can see the reflection of the Great Pyramid as well as swim in its shadow.

World famous people have walked through the hotel's doors over the years. In 1943 plans for Overlord, the invasion of Europe, were discussed there by Churchill and Roosevelt and arrangements were made for their meeting with Stalin in Teheran. It was from Mena House one day after tea that Churchill took Roosevelt to see the Sphinx for the first time. More recently, Presidents Sadat and Carter met at the hotel to formulate plans for the Camp David peace agreement in America. Film stars like Omar Sharif are habitués and the hotel acted as a background for the film of Agatha Christie's *Death on the Nile*. Shirley Maclaine has been a guest but insisted on spending part of one night in the Great Pyramid where the hotel hurriedly fixed up a makeshift room.

Mena House has its own golf course, at present only nine holes but soon to be enlarged. Beyond it is Mena Village, edged by a tree-lined canal. The next village, about two miles further towards the city, is Horraniya which has become famous these last few years because of its unusual rug factory. A building was set up for youngsters with no carpet making experience and they were given looms and coloured wools and shown how to weave. Then they were asked to make up designs of their own and weave them into a rug. They

The Nile at Aswan

Son-et-lumière at Abu Simbel

One of Abercrombie &
Kent's small cruise yachts,
the *Abu Simbel*

The Temple of Khnum in its
huge excavation at Esna

could use any subject they liked as long as it made a picture. The result was remarkable. Some children even imagined snow scenes which they could never have seen. As their skill increased many developed excellent technique and imagination. The gifted students remained, the rest went on to other occupations. Today Horraniya rugs are expensive and have been on exhibition in many European countries. Rosenthal of Germany used several of the rugs as a background for a china exhibition in London, for one of the Earls Court exhibitions. A team of girls together with their looms gave daily demonstrations.

At Sakkara you can visit many interesting sites, the most famous being the strange step pyramid of Zoser, the earliest of the Great Pyramids. It was designed by Imhotep, an architect of the Third Dynasty, who was also a brilliant statesman and skilled doctor. A recent cartoon shows a girl in Pharaonic costume with a bucket of water and scrubbing-brush cleaning one of the steps and looking with despair at the remainder!

To get back to reality, Imhotep's tomb has never been discovered. Professor Bryan Emery was convinced it was somewhere at the Sakkara site but, although he uncovered countless finds there including the golden image of Horus, he never found it. Although the professor is now dead his work is carried on and it is hoped that, one day, Imhotep's tomb will be unearthed. The Zoser Pyramid is unlike those at Giza in many ways: for instance its sides do not exactly face the cardinal points and it is rectangular in shape.

At Sakkara you can also explore the deep ruined Pyramid of Unis, the earliest one to contain religious inscriptions, which can be seen by the aid of neon lighting powered by a generator. This pyramid was excavated in 1881 at the expense of Thomas Cook the travel agent. Its original height was about 62 feet (19 m) and it measures 220 feet (67 m) at the base. There had been various attempts to break into it centuries ago and one of the predators, Ahmed the Carpenter, left his name inside in red paint. Ahmed is believed to be the same man who opened the Cheops Pyramid in 820 A.D. The strange thing about this ancient monument is that from the outside it does not look like a pyramid at all. It might be a craggy hill surrounded by stone rubble. You enter through a large hole at the base and it is almost a shock to find neat, tidy passages leading to the various chambers which look as if the illuminated walls had been painted only yesterday.

The Serapeum of the Apis Bulls is a labyrinth of large dark corridors where the animals, worshipped during their lifetime, were laid to rest when dead in mummified splendour. Whatever else you see at Sakkara, do not fail to see the tomb of Ti (pronounced tea) for its splendid walls are most exquisitely carved and still retain much of their colour. Ti was a court official of the Old Kingdom, young and handsome as can be judged by his statue in the Cairo

Step Pyramid at Sakkara. In front can be seen an early attempt at round columns keyed into a wall—dating from about 2700 B.C.

Antiquities Museum. On the north wall he is shown in a boat going through a papyrus thicket close to the bank where you can see fledglings being fed by parent birds in their nests. Other birds are sitting on their eggs. In a preceding boat, men are looking for hippopotami. You see a baby hippopotamus trying to climb onto his mother's back while another is trying to bite a crocodile. From Ti's boat his steersman is fishing. On the south wall, Ti and his lovely wife Neferhotpes are depicted watching animals being paraded before them for inspection. The cattle wear ceremonial collars and are led by leather leads, antelopes are restrained by their horns. Before Ti stands his steward checking the inventory on a papyrus scroll.

Memphis, the ancient capital of Egypt, lies between Sakkara and the Nile some 12 miles (19 km) south of Cairo. It was founded by Menes of the First Dynasty who built the great temple of Ptah, a serapeum, a temple to Isis and another to Ra. Here too were colossal statues of Ramses and several other pyramids. When Cairo became the capital of Egypt, most of these buildings were destroyed to provide material for the palaces there. The two large statues of Ramses survived. One is now in front of Cairo's main station while the other remains in Memphis. It is recumbent and has now been surrounded by an open air gallery to enable tourists to see and photograph it without trampling on it. Nearby is an eighteenth century alabaster sphinx re-erected exactly over the spot where it was excavated.

The Green Pyramids Hotel, tucked away off the Pyramids Road is about $2\frac{1}{2}$ miles (4 km) from the centre of Cairo. It is run by the Swiss Nova Park Group. It grew from an idea of Doctor Yussef Wahby, a famous actor who was about to retire and wished to live in a Swiss villa–but in Egypt. The result was a lavishly furnished house that might have arrived by magic carpet from a Swiss Alp. Wahby missed his friends and audiences and solved his problem by letting the Swiss firm of hoteliers build a hotel round his villa. Three new bedroom blocks have been squeezed into the landscape gardens of the villa and somehow seem to fit in with the original eccentric house. There are 72 rooms, de-luxe baroque suites, a poolside restaurant and the Bodega, a chalet-type restaurant with a rustic interior, offering international and Swiss specialities at any time of the day.

The Fayoum

Nearly 62 miles (100 km) south of Cairo is the nearest of Egypt's oases to the Nile valley. A straight tarmac road leads across the desert. Referred to sometimes as Egypt's National Park, it is the country's most fertile oasis and can be reached by bus. The greenery is unbelievably lush and one particular form of gardening there is rose growing, from which is prepared the rose water so popular throughout the Middle East. The Fayoum pigeon cotes are quite different from any others in Egypt and resemble small pyramids. As you drive to the Fayoum, with desert stretching for miles on either side, you can imagine how grateful the bedouin feel when they come upon an oasis after the arid sandhills. On the outskirts there are trees and at Kranis there is a little museum on the left and a small rest house where you can have a cooling drink or buy some of the Fayoum's produce such as fresh olives and honey.

The museum has several mummies, *ushabti* (devotional figurines) and in one cabinet there are many tiny cat Bast statues. She was worshipped as long ago as 3200 B.C. The people of the Delta, a region then frequented by snakes of many kinds, welcomed the wild cat which killed them. One myth says that Bast accompanied the Solar Boat through the regions of darkness and nightly gave battle to the serpent Apep, the enemy of Ra. Just inside the entrance of the museum there is a stone crocodile. The Greeks called the Fayoum 'Crocodilopolis' for it was also sacred to the crocodile god Sebek. There are beautiful examples of the famous 'Fayoum Portraits' in the Hellenistic style. A considerable number of them have been found in the area because the Ptolomies settled many Greek families here, calling it New Macedonia. Fourteen of the villages still bear their old Grecian names. The portraits are painted in the encaustic style (with the wax paint burnt in) and are vivid and lifelike. Some of the best examples are in the Antiquities Museum.

Just beyond the museum the road suddenly cuts right into the green of the oasis. On either side tall acacias, palm and eucalyptus trees throw dappled shadows. If you stop your car and listen you can hear the faint splashing of many water wheels. It is a great agricultural area and there is an impressive range of almond, apricot, orange, lemon, pomegranate, fig and olive groves. Grapes grow on bushes about two feet high and the white berries they produce are called 'fayoumi', a grape of medium size. Sugar cane grows high and you will see many rice paddies in between the irrigation canals. Following the plough or wading in the rice paddies are slim white egrets.

Medinet el Fayoum is the capital of the province and in the centre of a traffic island in the busiest part of the town, there is an obelisk erected by King Sesostris in the Twelfth Dynasty. It is 42 feet (13 m) high, made of granite and covered with pharaonic inscriptions. Other pharaohs of the same dynasty brought wealth to the city and their pyramids can be found in the outskirts while, far away in the desert, lie the old Greek cities from whose ruins came unique treasures of classical and biblical papyri.

The jewel of the Fayoum is Lake Karoun. Placid and smooth as mother-of-pearl it shimmers into the distance. The marshes surrounding it are full of bird life and there is constant chirping.Sometimes date palms and crops edge the water, at other places there is a fine white sand where fishing nets are spread to dry. European wildfowl tarry on the lake during their annual migration. Not only the sportsman but the ornithologist and naturalist find the lake entrancing, for it can produce every species of bird of prey, duck (including the rare marbled duck) pelicans, cranes and storks.

Recently opened is the Oberoi Auberge, a residential country club at the lake's edge. Originally King Farouk's hunting lodge, it has been remodelled into an unusual club with every modern amenity, including squash and tennis courts and riding stables, yet it retains much of its old lavish decor.

Heliopolis

Today, Heliopolis is a suburb some 6 miles (10 km) from the centre of Cairo. In Arabic it is called Masr al Gadida, meaning New Cairo. All that remains of the ancient part is the name and one obelisk. This is one of two made by Usertsen I in 2433 B.C., to stand before a temple in the biblical city of On. Joseph married a daughter of Potiphar, a priest of On. Later Cambyses razed the city and it was eventually rebuilt by the Greeks who christened it Heliopolis–City of the Sun.

Arab writers say that many statues remained in situ at the end of the twelfth century. The fabled phoenix was supposed to be reborn there every 500 years. Whatever the truth, all that remains now is the obelisk, but this is fascinating because it is the oldest in Egypt. It seems odd that the whole city succumbed to the desert save for this obelisk, which today is still in a remarkable state of preservation.

When the first Aswan Dam was finished in 1902, the event was as exciting to the Egyptians as the opening of the Suez Canal had been. For the first time the Nile had been harnessed. There was great confidence in the future. Towns and villages expanded and agriculture increased. During the next few years businesses of every kind boomed. One of the biggest deals was the sale by the Egyptian Government of 5000 acres (2025 hectares) of desert land north east of Cairo. Belgian money secured most of it and a railway line was built to link the site to the city. This was the rebirth of Heliopolis. Buildings rose one after the other, the most ambitious–intended at first to be a large casino like that in Monte Carlo–eventually became the Heliopolis Hotel.

Today, Heliopolis has wide boulevards, an arcaded shopping street, a sports club, spacious villas and luxury flats. The President has his villa there and there are several hotels in Heliopolis and at the nearby Cairo Airport. The El Salaam Hyatt has its own swimming pool and gardens. Its lobby is decorated in Georgian Wedgwood style. Only a few minutes away from the airport is the Heliopolis Sheraton. Its enormous marble-floored lobby has a fountain and there are seven different eating places. Apart from all the usual services there are several unexpected touches. You can hire a helicopter. There are courtesy buses into Cairo. Avis and Swissair have offices. There are library, conference and executive facilities, a jogging track and one of the restaurants–The Tent– reproduces the genuine atmosphere of an Egyptian village down to the baking of bread in clay ovens. There is even a very authentic English pub.

It has always seemed to me difficult to set up an English pub anywhere else but in Britain. Many countries have tried it, with limited success. The hardware can be exported but it is an exacting task to recreate the genuine atmosphere. Sheraton however, with 'The Swan' have been very successful here, even down to such details as an English phone box. Swans have always been a feature of English rivers. In earlier times they were a table delicacy and Chaucer writes of a luxury loving monk 'A fat swan loved he best of any roast.' Always a symbol of beauty, in Elizabeth I's time, it was the name of a theatre in London. Shakespeare was called the Swan on the Avon and it has been used as the name of various inns since the sixteenth century. One Englishman who frequently visits Cairo has been having his lunch and dinner regularly at The Swan pub since its opening. Like so many others, he enjoys the dark panelling, the chimney place, the raised platform with chairs and tables scattered about and the typical wooden bar. Recently he heard that a Swan Pub in north-east London was being redecorated and he managed to procure the old sign– naturally a painting of a swan. He presented it to the General Manager, Peter Tischmann, and it now hangs to bid visitors welcome thousands of miles from its original setting. Fortunately, swans themselves are not migratory birds. Incidentally, Peter Tischmann is such a perfectionist that he arranges in his King Tutankhamun Restaurant for the ladies to find fresh orchids in their napkins.

4

FOOD AND DRINK

Egyptians love good food and are known for their hospitality. If you are invited to an Egyptian dinner party for the first time, do not worry that there may be a course that you do not like. There will be so many tempting dishes on the table that you will be able to choose exactly what you want. Try a little of everything and please yourself. If this sounds extravagant it is the Egyptian way of life, and you can be certain nothing will be wasted. Unexpected guests may arrive, other members of the family drop in, special dishes may be sent to friends or relatives, and servants can take things to their families. Food will always be eaten by someone and never thrown away. Knowing this, do not eat too much if you are not hungry–as long as you enjoy yourself, your host will be happy.

One of the joys of travel is to taste new ways of cooking food. The Egyptians have several unusual dishes and you are sure to love some of them. You may even attempt some of them when you return home. Naturally, all the top class hotels offer international fare, so if you prefer that you know it is obtainable. Here are four recipes from four leading Cairo hotel chefs.

Daoud Pasha (for 6)
Ingredients

150g of butter	1 litre of stock
1kg rice	500g vermicelli
500g finely minced meat	500g peeled and sliced tomatoes
Salt, pepper or paprika	4 cloves of garlic
Flour, parsley	3 onions

Method
Put 150g of butter into a pan, add 2 finely grated onions and 3 cloves of garlic finely sliced. Fry to a golden colour. Add the tomatoes. Season with salt and pepper and leave to cook well for ½ hour. Add to the minced meat 1 clove of garlic and 1 small grated onion and some parsley. Mix well. Divide and shape the meat into small balls, roll in flour and fry in oil or butter. To prepare the rice and vermicelli first wash the rice and leave it to dry well. Fry the vermicelli in butter to a golden brown and remove from the pan. Then fry the rice in butter turning well until it is almost brown. Add the vermicelli and the stock. Bring back to the boil, cover the pan and place in the oven until well cooked. Take a deep dish and arrange the meat balls at the bottom. Put the rice

and vermicelli on top and press down firmly. Turn it all into a serving dish, pour the sauce over and serve hot.

Chicken with Hommos (for 4)
Ingredients
1200g chicken	160g dried chick peas
2 onions	2 cloves of garlic
120g butter	120g tomato purée
1 bouquet garni	250ml chicken stock
Salt and pepper	Flour

Method
Soak the chick peas thoroughly, preferably overnight. Cut the chicken into 8 pieces, season and roll in flour. Melt the butter and fry the onions, add garlic and chicken and sauté for 5 minutes. Add the tomato purée and again stir for 5 minutes. Add the stock and leave on a high flame until the chicken is cooked. Boil the chick peas in a separate pan, drain, add to the chicken and cook again for 5 minutes.

Rice Omar el Khayyam (for 6)
Ingredients
1kg rice	50g sultanas
25g butter	1 chopped onion
100g chicken or veal liver	1kg of kebab
500ml stock	

Method
Wash the rice and sauté in butter with chopped onion. Add stock to cover the rice and cook gently until it is soft. Fry separately sultanas and liver chopped and seasoned. Mix together with the rice and place in medium oven for 15-25 minutes. Serve with kebab. To make the kebab take 1 kilo of saddle mutton, bone it and cut into pieces, season with juice of 2 onions, 1 tomato and pepper and salt. Skewer and grill over charcoal for 5-10 minutes.

Ragout a l'Oriental (for 8)
Ingredients
100g finely chopped onion	10g finely chopped garlic
500g sliced mutton	500g peeled and sliced tomatoes
500g carrots	500g marrow
500g egg plant	500g ocra
500g French beans	Salt and pepper
25g butter	

Method
Fry onions and garlic in butter until brown. Add sliced mutton and fry until meat is half cooked. Add tomato, season with pepper and salt and leave to

simmer on a moderate flame. Slice all vegetables separately and fry in butter until each is half cooked. Arrange in a casserole a layer of one vegetable then a layer of mutton, then another vegetable until all are used up. Add remainder of the juice left from cooking the meat and place in moderate oven until cooked. Turn out onto a dish and serve hot.

The method of making kebab is included in one of the above recipes and it is popular in Egypt with kofta. This is spiced minced lamb, rolled into sausages and threaded on the skewer. Lamb and veal are the best Egyptian meats, beef can be tough and pork is not served in a muslim country.

All kinds of fish are delicious, from Nile bass to shrimps. Alexandria is famous for shell fish and sends them all over the country. Yoghurts are popular, especially one made with cucumber. You peel and slice the cucumber, add it to yoghurt with chopped mint or chives, and chill.

You may have tried your first Egyptian food on an EgyptAir aircraft on your way out as they serve some specialities. If you travel first class, not only are the meals delicious but your table is laid with an Egyptian cotton cloth with napkin to match. After your meal you will be invited to keep them both as souvenirs. A popular Egyptian dessert is Om Ali (Ali's Mother). Here is the recipe.

Ingredients

2¼ cups flour	6 cups milk
2 cups sugar	1 cup cream
½ cup raisins or nuts	1 egg
¼ teaspoon salt	½ cup water
1 tablespoon of samna (oil) for frying	

Method

Mix flour, salt and egg together, add water and make a soft dough. Divide it into 20 pieces, cover with a towel and let it rise for 20 minutes. Roll each piece out to the thickness of a coin and fry it to a light brown in the oil. Crumble 10 into a greased baking dish, add the raisins and top with remaining 10. Press down well. Pour the sugar into the boiling milk and stir until dissolved. Pour this into the baking dish and add the cream. Bake in a medium oven for 30 minutes and serve hot.

Egyptian bread is unleavened and therefore does not rise. It is shaped in flat thin rounds which can easily be torn either partly open to form a purse for fillings or completely in two when it is thin enough to cook in a slow oven to make melba toast.

Fresh vine leaves are used to make mashi. The leaves are blanched (they can even be bought ready for use in tins) and a mixture of minced lamb and seasoned rice is then rolled in them and cooked–delicious. When visiting Aswan you must try the local sun dried peanuts and dates. Also the kakade bush grows there, which is like a tea plant and has similar leaves. It is infused like tea and can be served iced or hot with or without sugar.

In Cairo there are houseboats moored along the Nile banks where you can lunch or dine. A recent addition to the eating-out scene is the introduction of cruising restaurants. Perhaps the best known is the Nile Pharaoh operated by Mena House Oberoi. You can enjoy first-class lunch or dinner cuisine with a constantly changing background.

If you are on a Nile cruise for several days you will certainly eat on board. Each place you dock, fresh fruit and vegetables are taken on. If you are on one of the large Sheraton boats complete with swimming pool, there are usually two sittings for meals and you choose the time that suits you best. In the evening there is often an elaborate buffet where you can serve yourself from a table of hot and cold dishes. If you have chosen to book on one of the smaller boats such as are operated by Abercrombie & Kent, you might almost be on a private yacht. You will not get the wide selection posible on the bigger boats but you will enjoy delicious meals conjured up by excellent chefs and such personal touches as safe ice made from mineral water.

If you happen to return mid-afternoon slightly jaded from a sightseeing tour, you will especially enjoy the freshly baked cakes and cookies served at tea time. After dinner, if there is no party or special entertainment, you can play bridge or patience, read a book from the library, go ashore or just sit on deck and order a drink from a well-stocked bar.

Drink

Although coffee is supposed to be the Egyptians' favourite drink and Turkish coffee is invariably offered by merchants when you shop, tea is just as popular especially with the fellaheen. If you have not had Turkish coffee before, remember not to stir it for it is very strong and the bottom of your tiny cup will be full of grounds. As the sugar is boiled with the coffee grains you have to say how much you want when you order it. There are three choices: without, with some and with a lot. With some, called mazboot, seems to suit most Europeans best.

Alcohol is technically frowned upon in a Muslim country but you will be able to obtain spirits, wines and beer easily at a price. A story goes that the late Aga Khan was asked by his hostess at a dinner party why he drank wine if he was a Muslim. 'I am the head of my sect' he replied, 'and when I drink wine it turns to water in my mouth!'

The vine was imported into Egypt from Asia thousands of years ago. The modern vineyards outside Alexandria are believed to be on the site of those at the time of Cleopatra and they produce some very pleasant wines. Due to the predictable sunny weather the growing conditions can be strictly controlled and watering is done as necessary by flooding troughs between the rows fed by canals. Consequently quality can be guaranteed. The vines are protected from desert winds by planting windbreaks of pine trees.

It is difficult to describe wines for other people but as a guide, the white wines range from the driest to the sweetest as follows: Village, Clos Matamir, Cru des Ptolemees (usually available), Nefertiti and Reine Cleopatra. Of the reds, Rubis d'Egypte is quite good and Muscat d'Egypte resembles a madeira. You will soon find your favourite. Of course, you can get French wines but they are very expensive.

Beer is readily available and the local one, Stella, rather like a lager, is refreshing served cold. The only problem, if indeed it is one, is that it only comes in large bottles, but then you can always share.

5

MINIA, BENI HASSAN
AND
TEL EL AMARNA

A Nile cruise package will normally include the flight out to Egypt and back, and Thomson Holidays have added the intriguing possibility of a trip one way in a British Airways Concorde. The cruises usually include some days sightseeing in Cairo at the beginning and end of the visit. The majority of cruises operate between Luxor and Aswan in Upper Egypt, or the reverse. However, several companies including Bales, Abercrombie & Kent, and Swan Hellenic offer longer cruises of ten to twelve days covering the whole distance between Cairo and Aswan or the return journey. Abercrombie & Kent in particular use smaller boats giving almost the atmosphere of a private yacht.

Guest lecturers of different nationalities or very knowledgeable Egyptian guides accompany the tours. Larger boats tend to do the shorter Aswan-Luxor cruises carrying bigger groups and again provide lecturer-guides who speak the appropriate languages. Many of these ships are operated by the big hotel companies such as Sheraton, Hilton and Oberoi and provide accommodation comparable to their hotel standards. (See Appendix 2 at the back of the book for names of operating companies). Joining and leaving the cruise ships within Egypt is normally arranged by air or rail.

As yet there there are no cruise ships on Lake Nasser as they cannot pass the High Dam but Sheraton and one or two other companies have plans in hand to assemble boats above the dam and this will enable tourists to cruise to Abu Simbel and other antiquities on the lake. At present you must fly from Aswan to Abu Simbel, but a road is being constructed along the side of the lake which will eventually reach Wadi Halfa in the Sudan and will make coach trips to Abu Simbel a possibility. The only boats on the lake at present are operated as a passenger service and are not designed for tourists.

Before embarking on the cruise and describing the various sites which you will visit, there are one or two further points to be made. In this book I have chosen to cruise from Cairo southwards to Upper Egypt: there are of course an equal number of cruises in either direction. Secondly, if you are young and adventurous, you can arrange a cruise in a native sailing craft, a felucca. Several firms will organize this for you, such as Wexas and Exodus Expeditions. It will be much cheaper; due to wind and current it cannot adhere to a fixed schedule. You will sleep under the stars and feed on local basic produce and sanitation will be on a bucket behind the bushes basis. You can even do a cruise without using a boat at all, travelling instead on a small bus alongside the river with Explorer Worldwide.

On your way to embark on the Nile after a few days in Cairo, it is surprising how familiar you will have become with the city. Perhaps it stems from your school days when you first learnt of the Pyramids, the Sphinx and the Antiquities Museum. You leave behind the busy streets, traffic jams, honking horns, pavements covered with parked cars and eddying dust. Yet you will remember endearing sights also; the patient donkeys three abreast tugging refuse carts to the city dumps, slowly trotting through traffic lights whether red or green; parked cars clad in well-fitted cotton covers reaching to the tyres to repel dust. The cheerful street vendors trying to attract your attention, offering flowers, newspapers or boxes of toilet tissues, weaving through the traffic but marvellously never getting knocked down. The amusing ready replies to questions asked by tourists: 'Why is the river called the Nile?' enquires a lady. 'It is named after the Nile Hilton' comes a quick response.

When you go aboard your ship, settle into your cabin and then go up on deck to watch the passing scene, again it seems familiar. The soaring hotels and the Corniche give way to riverside cafes, parkland, blocks of flats, villas and the tree lined streets of Maadi and Helwan. The Giza Pyramids can be seen in the distance on the east bank and later those at Sakkara.

As Cairo and its outskirts are left behind, the buildings vanish and the river banks on either side are luxuriant with trees and crops. The majority of Egyptians make their livelihood by farming. The Koran says that Man cannot exist without constant effort and this seems to be their philosophy. Because of the dry sunny climate and highly organized irrigation, the growth of crops is so rapid that the fellah is constantly tending the soil. Clad in his long cotton robe and small skull cap, there is no more picturesque sight along the Nile and canals than the one of the fellah working in the fields. He is lean and of medium height. Beneath straight eyebrows, his sunburnt face is thin with high cheekbones. Physically he still resembles the figures in the drawings on the temple walls.

Ploughing is done by the traditional yoke of oxen or buffalo. The plough, called a zahhafa, its point iron shod, is merely a long wooden pole or tree trunk. It does not pierce the soil deeply but sufficiently for the seed to take root and, such is the richness of the land, during the space of a year some four or five crops can be grown on the same plot. Invariably you will see graceful white egrets swoop downwards at the fellah's heels collecting worms from the freshly turned soil. These are the same scenes that delighted Anthony and Cleopatra. Even the typical lateen sails of the feluccas have not changed.

The staple food of the peasant is unleavened bread filled with 'fool', a type of haricot bean which is the hardiest of the Egyptian vegetables. He grows bercime, an emerald green clover, for his animals. First of all the soil is covered by some three inches of water and then the seed is sown broadcast. When the water has been absorbed into the ground the seed germinates on the surface and with little delay, sprouts its thin green stalk sunwards. It is sold by the growing area, the animals sometimes being brought to the bercime rather than the fodder to the animals.

The fellaheen women bring their laundry to the river's edge and gossip while they wash it. Although their menfolk wear traditional galabiehs of white, grey or striped cotton, the women love vivid colours such as red and tangerine which draw the eye of ship's passengers, although they seem to remain unaware of it. Many older women wear a black robe over their coloured dresses. Such domestic scenes pass by the tourists as if on a television screen. You will see them bend down to the water, fill a copper or clay vessel to the brim and, without spilling a drop, place it on a cloth pad on their heads. As the bottom is rounded it balances perfectly. Then they walk home with a grace and dignity which has been handed down by their forebears. A glamourous touch, denoting the wealth of her family, is sometimes suggested by gold or gilded coins suspended from the veil covering the lower part of her face. You may get a glimpse of a silver anklet or even of a gold one, perhaps inherited or given at her wedding. Tourists can seldom buy antique anklets for they are venerated far more highly than wedding rings or bracelets.

The great curse of the fellaheen is bilharzia, a more malignant disease than malaria or dysentery. It can be cured but unfortunately recurs. It is caused by worms that thrive in the mud of the irrigation canals. The bug penetrates the skin and settles in the kidneys and liver where it devitalizes even the strongest of men. Great efforts have been made to stamp it out but even emptying the canals and catching millions of the worms by dragging the mud with nets only cuts the menace without eliminating it. It is a slow battle, but research work is carried on to discover methods of controlling the disease. Obviously it is unwise for the tourist to go barefoot.

The old saying of Herodotus that Egypt is the gift of the Nile is still true. Fruit and vegetable terraces edge straight down into the river and patient buffaloes slowly turn water wheels. As well as the modern diesel driven pump you will see peasants still using two other ancient methods for raising the water for irrigation. The 'shadoof' comprises a long pole pivoted on a trestle with a bucket on a rope at one end counterbalanced at the other with a lump of mud. The operator lowers the bucket into the water by pulling the rope downwards and then raises the full bucket and empties it into a channel. The Archimedean screw consists of an inclined pipe dripping down into water with a large corkscrew running down the centre. This is rotated by turning a handle and thus lifts up the water.

The river level is now meticulously controlled by the Aswan High Dam but you can sometimes see a man in a felucca using a midra, a long pole, to take soundings. Fortunately the prevailing wind on the Nile is from the north so the feluccas are able to sail on most days of the months against the north flowing current. It takes a skilled pilot to thread between shoals in some places. The river is nowhere very deep and occasional bumps on the bottom and, rarely, running aground are possibilities which are not dangerous snd should not alarm you on your cruise. Your ship is never out of sight of land and normally cruises for part of each day, mooring when it reaches towns, sites or at night to enable you to go ashore.

During the hottest part of the year, harvesting grain and other farming activities often take place at night for, when the moon is full, it is nearly as bright as day and the air is cool. Rural life ceases as you draw near to Minia, 155 miles (250 km) south of Cairo and probably your first stop. Tall trees are reflected in the water as you climb a flight of stone steps leading to a splendid corniche. To the right they extend into a gracious park. On the far side of the corniche there are a couple of hotels and a museum.

Minia University is well known for its faculty of arts and human sciences. Among other faculties are those of agriculture and medicine. There are also a number of factories in Minia which is the capital of a province, among them a cotton spinning mill, cattle food plant and a sugar refinery. The main street is tempting and there is a souk.

A most interesting museum is at Mallawi some $7\frac{1}{2}$ miles (12 km) from Minia. It is a joy to visit not only to see several unusual exhibits but also because it is spotlessly clean. Each gleaming cabinet has a card in English describing the contents as well as one in Arabic. One room has numerous ibis statues of the Graeco-Roman period 300 B.C., the most important one made of gilded wood with bronze legs and hindquarters. It holds its beak over a little goddess protectively. Three small wooden coffins contain ibis mummies. Another room has human mummies with mirrors arranged so that you can see the bottoms of the sarcophagi as well as the tops and sides. Two of them are unusual in that they have large eyes and eyebrows painted on the sides as if the mummies were regarding you from within their coffins. One cabinet may claim your attention as it contains plaster masks displaying elaborate hairstyles. Such wigs were often worn over shaven heads. Small ibis statues are quite beautiful, some wrapped in linen, others with tiny statues of Horus on their knees. One has a bared breast and is suckling a baby Horus. If you look closely you will note that it appears to wink at you. A reddish coloured animal resembling a chow dog wears an exquisite charm bracelet as a collar. Upstairs in the Mallawi museum there are collections of amphorae and Roman oil lamps. Samples of rugs from the Graeco-Roman period have interesting designs.

Some 12 miles (20 km) from Mallawi you can visit Tunah el Gebel, a desert area with precipitous hills. Here there are some very interesting tombs, not in the pyramid or deep shaft manner of the Pharaonic dynasties but more like the 'house' tombs in Syria at Palmyra. These Graeco-Roman tombs are not meant to be hidden from human eyes but to be visited and admired. The most impressive is that of Petosiris, built at the beginning of the Macedonian period about 300 B.C. Petosiris was chief priest to Thoth at Hermopolis. You enter through a vestibule the facade of which has four columns with floral capitals. These were painted in red, blue and turquoise and have retained their colours inside but outside have been bleached by the sun. The inner walls of the tomb are inscribed with the wise sayings of Petosiris and portray him with his wife talking to their family and priests. Their Greek robes look incongruous among the reliefs showing Pharaonic clothing. Coppersmiths and other metal workers are pictured at work. The actual burial chamber is in a vault but the coffin, inlaid with hieroglyphic inscriptions, is in the Cairo Antiquities Museum.

The most romantic tomb is that of Isidora, dated about 120 B.C. Apparently she was sailing across the Nile to visit her lover who was awaiting her on the other bank and waved to her. She stood up in joyous anticipation of their reunion and waved back to him, lost her balance and fell into the water. As she was unable to swim and nor could anyone else nearby, she drowned. Isidora's story has a Romeo and Juliet flavour and many people have been touched by it. In recent years the late Taha Hussein, the famous Egyptian minister of education who, although blind, was a remarkable man, had a rest house built nearby. When he visited the tomb he arranged that, whenever he stayed at his villa, candles should be lit in niches in Isidora's tomb as a gesture to her memory. He believed her drowning must have been one of the earliest cases of a maiden dying for love.

Beni Hassan

Back on the Nile you wend your way to Beni Hassan. After the modern corniche at Minia and the sandy stretches of Tunah el Gebel, it is completely different at Beni Hassan. Here you moor alongside a sandy bank where a long line of donkeys awaits your arrival, each held by a man who helps you to mount. If you prefer to walk rather than ride you can easily keep up with the column of donkeys along a flattish sandy trail. After about half an hour you come to the base of a mountain. Here you dismount and begin to climb some 200 steps. As they are divided into short flights with flat ground in between, it is not as arduous as it sounds. However it may not be wise for those unaccustomed to taking much exercise to climb as there are no railings.

At the summit you arrive on flat ground again to be confronted by a long row of rock tombs, about forty in number. Only a few are open to the public and of those to the north, numbers 2 and 17 are the most commonly visited. All are famous for the light they throw on the customs and manners of ordinary everyday life in ancient Egypt. From this ridge you get a wonderful view downward across the Nile valley and can appreciate why this magnificent site was chosen as a final resting place. Most of the tombs which are open are now illuminated by fluorescent lighting powered by portable generators so that you can see the interior decoration easily.

Porticos lead in through fluted pillars known as Greek-Doric which were however designed centuries before they were used in Greece. The columns, many of which are damaged or missing, divide each tomb into aisles and there is often a niche in the far wall for the statue of a god or goddess. The most interesting feature of these tombs to my mind is the wall paintings. These are done line upon line over whole walls almost like the pages of a book and they convey a vast amount of information.

Tomb 2 is that of Ameni, governor of the sixteenth nome in Egypt during the reign of Usertsen I. He was hereditary prince of the district and held the office of priest to various gods and goddesses. Pictures show the working of flint and metal, the making of beer, of bows, pottery, stone vessels, the ways of ploughing, treading of corn, reaping, wine making, the manufacture of rope, the netting of both fish and birds and games of different kinds including wrestling. The latter scene is famous and is thought to be one of the earliest surviving pictures of this sport. Many wrestlers have come to study it.

The most colourful tomb interior at Beni Hassan is 17, that of Khata who was once overseer of the Eastern Desert and governor of the nome of Meh. Two rows of columns might have been painted yesterday for they are still a glowing red, yellow and blue. It is difficult to decide which of the tomb paintings you admire most in these fascinating frescoes of the past. Gaiety is not forgotten for you will see banquets and festivals–and also intimate scenes such as going to the barber or cutting the toe nails! Cruelty and sorrow are there too; floggings, killings, weeping and mourning.

Time passes quickly at Beni Hassan and going down the flights of steps you will see your donkeys waiting patiently below to return you to your floating hotel.

Tel el Amarna

Some 40 miles (65 km) south of Minia you come to the important site of Tel el Amarna. Immense areas have been excavated at this location and have revealed the ancient capital which replaced Thebes for a time and came to be known as Akhen-Aton, the Horizon of the Sun. It was founded after the death of Amenhotep III (1411-1375 B.C.) whose widow, Queen Tiyia, encouraged her son, Amenhotep IV, to give precedence to the Sun-God Ra rather than other gods. The Queen was a commoner's daughter but a woman of forceful personality.

The young Pharaoh built a temple at Thebes to Ra under the name of Aton, the Sun Disc, the deity behind the sun who gives heat and light to the world. He thus swept aside the worship of Ammon together with the other gods and goddesses. This outraged the priests who rebelled and the Pharaoh therefore decided to abandon Thebes and, with his followers, build a new capital elsewhere. Good fortune was with him for, having sailed some 250 miles (422 km) down the Nile, he found a perfect place which it is said 'belonged to no

Luxor Temple. Note the minaret of the Abu Hagag mosque in the middle distance

An old Coptic church on the east bank of the Nile approaching Cairo

The Muhammad Ali mosque at the Citadel

An engraving of the Colossi of Memnon during a Nile flood, done at around the turn of the century by the Scots artist David Roberts

god or goddess, no prince or princess and of which no man could claim ownership.'

The site chosen was a great semi-circle of sand about 25 feet (8 m) above the Nile on the east bank. Edged by limestone cliffs and about three miles in width, it resembled a vast theatre.

While the city was under construction, Amenhotep changed his name to Akhnaton, 'the Aton is satisfied'. He was joined by thousands of followers from Thebes and instructed his architect Bek to procure red granite and alabaster for his palace and temples. Hundreds of brick makers were unceasingly at work moulding sun-dried mud bricks for the houses and so the new capital grew. Few traces remain of the great temple to Aton today, although it is known that it was 2409 feet (734 m) long and 902 feet (270 m) wide, so you can imagine how impressive it was. A series of tablets were carved in the cliffs and one which is often reproduced in books survives and shows Akhnaton and his wife, the beautiful Nefertiti, accompanied by their little daughters holding up their arms in veneration to the sun. An inscription on it commemorates the founding of the city. There are similar murals in the excavated tombs. The family scenes are all charming and in many of them the royal couple are pictured offering sacrifices to the sun whose rays often terminate in slender hands held out to bless. For the first time the stylized figures of royalty changed to life-like images.

Akhnaton remains one of the most fascinating of the pharaohs. Within his reign he changed his royal name, his capital, the artistic style of the temple and its wall reliefs. Most interesting of all is his cult of monotheism, centuries before our own beliefs were crystallized. Although 1000 years in advance of our own religions, many of his hymns of praise are similar to those in the Bible and the Koran. Thus:

Thou appearest resplendent on the horizons of the heavens,
thou living sun who wast the first to live. Thou arisest
on the eastern horizon and fillest the earth with thy beauty.
All the flocks are content in their pastures. The trees
and herbs become green, the birds flutter in their nests
and lift up their wings to praise thee. All creatures leap
upon their feet; all that flutter and fly live when thou arisest for them.

Nefertiti seemed the perfect queen for Akhnaton. She was not only beautiful and intelligent but also believed fervently in the new religion. There is a delightful granite head of her in the Cairo Antiquities Museum but it pales into insignificance when compared to her world famous 'Green Head'. This was excavated in 1912 at Tel el Amarna by a German Egyptologist, Dr Ludwig Boregart and is in the Berlin Museum. During the Second World War, the lovely head was encased in glass wool and hidden with other treasures in a cave in the Harz mountains. An American G.I. discovered it in 1945 and so for the second time it was resurrected and is now back in the

Replica of the head of Queen Nefertiti, wife of Tutankhamun, in West Berlin Museum

Berlin Museum. I saw it on display in the Wiesbaden Museum thirty years ago in a glass cabinet alone in a large room. People were passing by the cabinet slowly. No one talked. It is in truth breathtakingly beautiful. Beneath sweeping black eyebrows, one eye is lovely but the other is shown white for Nefertiti had a form of cataract. It is strange that this slight disfigurement does not detract from the beauty of the head.

One of Nefertiti's daughters was to marry Tutankhamun and, when the latter eventually became pharaoh, he returned with his Queen to Thebes and the old gods and goddesses. Tel el Amarna became a ghost city and gradually vanished. Yet fortunately digging still continues and more of this strange interlude in history will come to light.

Assiut

Assiut, 236 miles (380 km) from Cairo on the west bank, like so many towns along the Nile, has a beautiful tree-lined corniche where river passengers go ashore. Its barrage, built in 1898, formed part of the old Aswan Dam system for regulating the level of the Nile. It is the capital of the province of the same name and the birthplace of President Mubarak. The main part of the city, which has a population of nearly a quarter of a million, lies back from the Nile near the foot of a mountain and is really on an island formed by a branch of the river. There is a modern shopping centre and also a delightful souk where you can watch craftsmen at work. Assiut is known for its gold jewellery. Its great pride is its university. The buildings are in a large campus with lawns and flower gardens. The agricultural faculty is particularly impressive and the veterinary section has all kinds of animals housed under ideal conditions. A lake blending in with the landscape is in reality a fish hatchery.

A unique place to visit, easily accessible although halfway up a mountain side, is the Convent of the Virgin Mary. A roadway winds upwards to the convent precincts. Once inside you feel you have stepped back centuries. The main chapel can be reached by descending a staircase into a long dark cave. When your eyes have adjusted to the semi-darkness you enter the chapel which is enclosed by mushrabia panels. Behind the simple altar, hang ancient biblical paintings. More are behind the screens, through which a little light filters so that they can also be seen. They are most impressive; one of Christ being taken down from the cross is thought to be over 1000 years old.

If you sit for a while on one of the benches which act as pews, it is interesting to note that the rough stone cave-ceiling contrasts completely with the floor which is smooth and shining from people walking on it for centuries. There are three fonts, their covers being made in the form of crosses. Down through the years, numerous families have brought their children to be Christened in this ancient Coptic place of worship.

Since Nile cruises began, their duration has always varied to cater for different tastes. Today the trip between Luxor and Aswan taking four or five days is the most popular, but twenty years ago Assiut to Aswan in ten days was preferred. Thomas Cook, the founder of the company of the same name, opened his first Egyptian tourist office at Shepheards Hotel in Cairo in 1873. In those days a visitor had to pay in cash as he went along. Cook wrote back to his office in London that he had offered to pay the Egyptians by cheque or bankers draft for steamer accommodation. They had refused to accept either and, in the end, he had emptied a bag of 1300 gold sovereigns onto the office floor! Inevitably Cook had to find an answer to this and he was the first tour operator to offer the return ticket and hotel accommodation coupons. The company still uses the word coupon for its cable address.

Most tour operators today are tactful and diplomatic but this did not apply at the turn of the century and no one was more annoyed than Thomas Cook if his plans went awry. On one of his Nile trips, a delay was caused by his boat running onto a sandbank and by the time Assiut was reached, the lock passing the barrage was closed for the night. Cook was in a hurry to get to Cairo and was determined not to spend the night at Assiut. He sent an urgent message to the engineer in charge, asking that the lock gates be opened. The engineer, who was a Scot, refused. Cook finally got his way but only after a furious argument.

On the other hand, when Khedive Ismail took a trip up the Nile with the Khedivah, Thomas Cook made the arrangements and travelled with the royal couple himself. He enjoyed telling the story of his first meeting with the Khedivah. She and her ladies-in-waiting were towed in a luxuriously fitted barge behind the Khedive's private dahabeah. The royal party spent pleasant days visiting the temples, the ladies always going separately. At each landing stage the Khedive always threw largesse from sacks of copper coins. As Cook was coming back to the dahabeah after a walk one evening in Luxor he saw the ladies, attended by a tall Sudanese guard, on their way back from Karnak temple. He hurriedly averted his eyes so as not to embarrass the vice-regal harem but to his astonishment, the Khedivah herself came up to him and engaged him in conversation in a most charming way by saying: 'I have always desired to meet the great Mr Cook.' She was only lightly veiled and very beautiful. Thomas Cook ever after declared himself a most respectful and profound admirer.

Khedive Ismail and Thomas Cook were to have further business on the Nile–but not as pleasant as their sightseeing trip together. Towards the end of his reign, Ismail had many troubles in Egypt and the Sudan. There was an alarming rise in the slave traffic from the Sudan and a religious leader there was conducting a vicious crusade. Mohammed Ahmed, born in Dongola in 1843 and calling himself the Mahdi (he who must be obeyed) had acquired many disciples who were prepared to follow him to the death. He claimed that contact with Christians had caused decadance among the faithful and that he was deputed by God to rid the earth of them. Villages fell one after the other as his savagery increased. Ismail was prevailed upon to appoint a British

Governor General to the Sudan. He chose the intrepid General Charles George Gordon, who had made a great name for himself in China and was known as 'Chinese Gordon'.

Initially he thought of reaching Khartoum by using the Suez Canal and going overland into the Sudan. But then John Mason Cook, Thomas's son, was commissioned to take the General, his men and supplies, up the Nile. They came from Alexandria by rail to embark. Emir Abdul Shakour, a former ruler of the Sudan, was to join the same convoy. He held back departure somewhat while his mountains of luggage and twenty three wives got aboard. He caused yet more delay because his dress uniform had been left behind and had to be retrieved. Finally the convoy got under way upstream. The boats had to be hauled by hand through the cataracts.

Gordon's first job on arrival in Khartoum was to evacuate as many Europeans as possible. He succeeded partially but then the capital was besieged by the Mahdi's forces. The General held on heroically for several months praying for the arrival of the relief force which he knew would come. He never gave up but was killed two days before it came within sight of Khartoum. His corpse was decapitated and the head sent to the Mahdi.

However, his death was to be avenged. A cavalry officer in the relieving force was none other than Lieutenant-Colonel Horatio Kitchener–later to become Kitchener of Khartoum. He served in Palestine and Cyprus after Gordon's murder but then returned to Egypt where he became Sirdar of the Egyptian army and remained until he had achieved the reconquest of the Sudan. His greatest triumph came in 1898. It is not often that tour operators arrange transport for expeditionary forces but Thomas Cook's fleet had been rebuilt and was requisitioned to transport the forces that Kitchener needed for the return to the Sudan. At Omdurman, he routed the Mahdi and his dervishes and totally destroyed his power. On board one of the boats in the fleet was a young officer called Winston Churchill.

1984 marked the centenary of General Gordon's death and Thomas Cook arranged a special cruise to commemorate the event and the part played in it by Cooks a century ago. It was a ten day trip from Aswan to Cairo which included a fancy dress ball on board and another in Cairo. One of the two ships used was Sheraton's Tut, at present the largest boat on the Nile, which is just able to squeeze through the locks. A television team recorded the voyage which was shown in Britain early in 1985.

6

ABYDOS TEMPLE
AND
DENDERAH

Leaving Assiut and its rumbling barrage behind how can one forget such passing cameos as I saw one midday? An engaging old gentleman with long white beard wearing a turban and striped galabie was sailing along in his felucca smoking his 'hubbly bubbly' pipe. He passed a friend in another felucca who was trying hard to calm a fractious donkey, uneasy at being ferried across the river. A third felucca was piled high with clay pots full of honey, probably en route to market. This boat was in the sole charge of a small boy while his elderly relative slumbered in the stern.

Once through the barrage you slide along the river between palm tree lined banks, stark yellow cliffs, huddled villages and narrow fields. Men busily till the sloping terraces and women shepherd flocks of sheep, not by driving them from behind as we do in the West but by leading them. Egyptian sheep are attractive except for their fat, cumbersome tails. As the camel stores food and drink in his extra stomach, so these sheep store extra food in their tails. At market, sheep tail fat is the cheapest part of the carcase.

The buffalo is always in evidence for he helps the fellah wherever there is arable land, turning water wheels, tilling the soil and giving milk which is purer than that of the cow, for the buffalo is more disease resistant and is not inclined to tuberculosis. If you see these animals when being scrubbed down in the Nile at the end of their day's work, you will realize that they enjoy it. One evening near Mallawi, I was driving with friends along the bank of a wide canal. It seemed extraordinary how every creature kept to its own section of ground. Each beast had a mound of fresh green bercime to munch and about as much space as it would have in a stable. Each lot was separated only by tiny mud barriers 6 inches high, yet not one animal stepped out of its own 'kingdom'. One or two regarded us idly as we passed, their black noses shining like patent leather in the slanting sunlight. The egrets at this time of day leave their furrowed fields and rice paddies, to settle in a few favourite trees for the night, weighing the branches down so that in the fading sunset, the trees seem to be laden with large white flowers.

It is strange that the fellah should remain near the Nile village where he was born and have no desire to roam, when his brother the bedouin leads a nomadic life. The latter has always had a romantic appeal for the visitor but it

Bedouin women in traditional dress

is the fellah who is the mainstay of Egypt and, during Roman times, helped fill the 'granary of Rome'.

Tourists who look for a sunset as background for camels plodding along a technicolour skyline will not be disappointed. They can be seen almost any evening, for the camel is as important to the fellah as to the bedouin. He helps with ploughing and other farm work and carries the produce to the country markets. He is still a vital part in the economy of the country. He holds his head in such a disdainful manner because, it is said, although Man knows ninety-nine names for Allah, the camel knows the hundredth! The weight he

Donkey mother and foal near the river bank

can carry his phenomenal and his slithering cushion-footed gait enables him to plod with equal ease over the burning streets of the villages and towns or with the sand tugging at his heels in the desert. Without him the bedouin could not exist for the skin provides his tent and leather, the wool his rugs and bernous and dried camel dung his fuel. The camel possesses more endurance than any other creature and will not flag until he at the end of his tether. However once that point is reached nothing will resuscitate him, hence 'the straw that broke the camel's back'.

Abydos

The temple of Abydos on the west bank lies some 6 miles (10 km) from Baliana which is a busy riverside town. Here you dock and are taken by car or bus to the site. Baliana's streets are narrow and you brush by other tourist buses, honking cars, bicycles, laden camels and donkeys in the main street. Small shops line both sides, many of them frontless with fresh fruit and vegetables temptingly displayed. Shoe shops are much in evidence. Glancing through an old guide book, I noted that an hotel near the station was only recommended 'in an emergency'!

Suddenly, the din of the town is left behind, the pavements give way to canals and you are in the countryside with palm and acacia trees edging crops.

Fishing at night

Fellaheen look up from their labours and give friendly waves as you pass by. Gradually the greenery yields to the desert and you come to the temple.

Abydos stands in isolation, one of the most beautiful monuments in Egypt. Its ancient name was Thinis, famous as the birthplace of Menes and reputed burial place of Osiris, God of the Underworld and Resurrection. The temple became second only to those at Thebes. The Royal Tombs of Egypt's First and Second Dynasties are here, for everyone of importance wished to be laid to rest near the god so that graves reached to the outer walls and beyond. This is in complete contrast to the Pharaohs who wished no one to discover their burial vaults in the Valley of the Kings. Among the famous buried here are King Djer of the First and King Sethos I of the Nineteenth Dynasties. The latter made doubly sure of protection in the after life by having a rock tomb built at Thebes as well!

You enter the precincts along a great ramp or up steps on either side of which are large hollows which long ago were libation pools. The temple is dedicated to seven gods and there are seven vaulted knaves lying east and west ending in seven sanctuaries and communicating with two enormous halls running north and south. The are also several small chambers, one being the Holy of Holies where images of the gods could be placed. In Pharaonic times, two famous Osiris symbols were kept in the temple sanctum; one a bundle of golden flower stems and the other a large golden sceptre, the top of which was carved with a face and crowned with two ostrich feathers. Two cobras coiled above the forehead and the whole was studded with precious gems and blue faience.

The daily ritual of the high priest is described on the walls of Abydos thus. Before entering the temple, the priest would purify himself by washing in the sacred pool within the temple boundaries. He then lit a small fire to fill his censer with glowing charcoal. Sprinkling incense over it he would take it to the shrine where the figure of the god had been alone all night. He broke the clay seal of the door, walked in quietly and prostrated himself on the floor. He then arose to present honey or a small statue of Truth to the deity. Next, chanting and holding incense before him, he encircled the god four times. With great reverence he would lift the statue from its shrine, unfold its wrappings and anoint it with unguents. Placing it on a mound of consecrated sand representing the desert from which the sun rose each morning, he sprinkled it with holy water from fragile vessels and, having bathed its mouth with three different kinds of *natron*–a preservative solution–painted its eyelids with green and black cosmetics. Finally, the jewels were replaced and the god was invested with the royal insignia. It was then put back in its shrine and, having cleansed the altar, he covered it with fresh food and wine. The last act was to reseal the door and, intoning mystic chants, remove all traces of his footsteps and leave the Holy of Holies.

The temple walls are covered with bas reliefs and hieroglyphics and although they seem confusing at first, you soon learn to distinguish what some of them mean. For instance, gods can be recognized by their headdresses. Emblems of rule, sovereignty and dominion are represented by the crook, sceptre and flail. The Key of Life looks like the Christian cross save that it has a loop at the top. The cartouche or seal, an oblong with the personage's name carved within it, is seen again and again. Fortunately, most figures and scenes speak for themselves. At Abydos Seti I and his son, Ramses II tell their life stories in remarkable fashion.

The temple walls commissioned by Seti were called by Strabo, the Greek geographer, 'The Memnonium' and are generally considered to be the peak of perfection in this art. The Pharaoh gave his talented artists every facility and encouragement. They are unlike the sculptures of Ramses II, the great warrior who followed him, who insisted on incisive, definite lines emphasizing power and determination. When Seti died and his son became Pharaoh, he had the remaining walls covered with memorials to his father. Fate has been kind in Seti's part of the temple, for much of the beautiful colouring remains. The seventh nave was built to the glory of Seti himself. The walls depict the Pharaoh adoring himself as a god and being carried in procession by the gods themselves. Another is a carving of Seti offering an image of truth to Osiris. The modelling of the tiny figure in the outstretched palm of the Pharoah's hand is in itself exquisite. Then there is Seti proffering wine to Horus, about to place a brilliantly bejewelled collar around the neck of a god or Isis holding the Key of Life to Seti's lips. In yet another, Seti holds a little bat in his hand. If the fingers uncurled, it would surely dart away.

In a roofless antechamber, Seti is shown teaching his son how to lasso a wild bull. On a wall in a long gallery you can see the famous tablet of Abydos, that amazing catalogue of the seventy-six dynastic kings of ancient Egypt. Egyptologists have found this genealogical tree most helpful and from it know that many Pharaonic tombs have not yet been uncovered. Although the tablet is not a comprehensive list and does not give the names of the Pharaohs before the unification of Upper and Lower Egypt, it has proved to be a unique key to the past.

Motioning towards the seventy-six royal cartouches are two regal figures, one being Seti I and the other his son Ramses II. The King wears the double crown of Egypt while clasped about his neck is a jewelled collar. Wide bracelets are fastened about his arms at the wrists and above the elbows. A knee-length pleated skirt is drawn in at the waist over which flows a fine transparent outer skirt, falling to the ankles. The high arched feet are bare. One hand gestures gracefully with open tapering fingers towards the Pharaonic list while the other holds a rod at the end of which a modelled hand clutches a tiny bowl of incense.

Two corridors of burial vaults within the temple grounds have been uncovered in recent years. Digging still continues but unfortunately the water table has risen considerably since the construction of the High Dam at Aswan so that it is becoming very difficult to continue the work.

The roof of the temple is unique in Egypt. Immense stones were laid not flat but on their sides, across from pillar to pillar. Arches were then cut through these slabs of stone and decorated with sculptures and hieroglyphics.

Hathor Temple

Back on the Nile you cruise to see one more temple before arriving at Luxor ; the Hathor temple at Denderah. It is often overlooked because of its proximity

Special post-box once used by Mariette and Petrie to exchange notes on their excavations and finds at Abydos

ιo Abydos and Thebes, yet is has one of the most striking facades of any temple. Napoleon thought it was the most beautiful one in Egypt. En route you pass beneath the largest bridge in Egypt at Sohag, a town of some 48,000 inhabitants. The bridge is about 2200 feet (670 m) long with a middle swinging section for navigation and was built in 1953.

Denderah is 39 miles (64 km) north of Luxor on the west bank. We went ashore and walked along a sandy bank for a quarter of a mile until we reached a roadway where an air-conditioned bus awaited us. After a 3 mile drive we came to the temple, one of the best preserved in the country. Rebuilt in Roman times it stands alone: its impressive pylon pierced by six columns with Hathor heads as capitals. As we stood looking at it an old-fashioned post box was pointed out to me in a wall, put there at the turn of the century. Mariette, the French Egyptologist and Flinders Petrie, his English counterpart, used to leave papers in it to keep in touch with each other about their latest work.

Hathor, Goddess of Love, was known under many names and symbols in ancient Egypt. Her titles included Mistress of the Gods, Lady of the Sycamore, Hathor of Thebes and Lady of the West. She represented the female power in nature, wife of the Sun-God himself and gave sustenance to Man on earth and supposedly during the dangerous journey through the Underworld.

Gate of the Temple at Denderah

Sometimes she wore a sycamore emblem on her head with her hands full of flowers and fruit. At other times she was seen in the form of a cow with yet another Hathor symbol between the horns, the lunar disc backed by two large ostrich feathers.

As you enter through the large pylon (gateway) the lintel overhead is sculptured with the wings of Horus. You come into a large hall with a wide central aisle and three rows of pillars on each side. Instead of lotus flower or papyrus capitals, each pillar–of which there are twenty four–is topped by a Hathor head. Sandwiched between each head and the ceiling are replicas of the goddess suckling a babe. Turquoise blue still adheres to the broad foreheads, though much of the other colouring has peeled. Gods and sacred barks are depicted in the ceiling.

The stone floor is uneven and care is needed to avoid holes when looking upwards. An opening in the wall leads into a larger hall where small chambers go off to left and right. The sanctuary is in the middle. In this sanctuary, a beautiful fresco shows Hathor being proffered incense by a young pharaoh. It is held out to the goddess on a perfectly carved hand at the end of a slender staff. All temple drawings show incense being offered in this way so that the human may not come into too close proximity with the deity.

One of the small chambers has its roof design showing the goddess's body edging three sides. Sunrays issue from the groin and strike a sun disc, symbol of Ra, on the fourth side. From an antechamber you can ascend a shallow staircase to a small shrine dedicated to Osiris called the Temple on the Roof. Again the ceiling is of interest having in the centre a full face carving of Hathor as a woman and in a corner a blackened zodiac. The latter is a replacement by Muhammad Ali who had the original cut out and sent to Paris as a gift in 1821. It is now in the Louvre. The walls are covered with reliefs of a mummified pharaoh being brought back to life by the occult powers of the God of Fertility.

Back at ground level again, there is a sort of crypt, a long narrow passage beneath the flooring. You have to descend a flight of steps and take a torch or be given a candle. It is not very high and you will need to bend if you are tall. There are exquisite cameos which have retained their colouring and are in excellent condition. Here you can see the god Horus with feathers that look real enough to touch and a delightful portrait of Cleopatra nursing Caesarian. A king and queen are seated on thrones. I have only visited this unique place once and last time I was there the crypt was closed because people had been frightened by bats.

The temple walls inside and out are inscribed with the names of Roman Emperors. One of the outer walls is very famous for it boasts a carving of Cleopatra, Caesar and their son Caesarian. Cleopatra is in profile so that one cannot see her fatal beauty which so captivated Caesar and Mark Anthony. Nevertheless, it is one of the most photographed walls in Egypt.

You cross the courtyard to see the Mammisi or House of Giving Birth, built by Augustus. A square building, it is much larger than the Temple on the Roof. On its inner walls the Goddess Hathor is shown as a woman in the various stages of giving birth.

Both at Kom Ombo temple not far from Denderah and in the Fayoum, crocodiles were feared and worshipped. They were identified with Sobek, the god with the crocodile head. In contrast it is reputed that, in ancient days, the people of Denderah could swim in the Nile without being attacked and had no fear of them. The Romans wished to exhibit crocodiles in their own country and invited a number of Denderah Egyptians to attend them. The strange entourage went to Rome where a pool was built to hold the reptiles. It was edged with a platform where the Egyptians would drag the crocodiles from the water in nets so that the Romans could see them.

7

LUXOR

Along the highway of the Nile the obelisk and columns of Luxor temple come into view even before you dock beside the corniche bow-to-stern with other passenger steamers. You step ashore at about the same place as did Anthony and Cleopatra. Above its mighty columns you may look a second time in disbelief for, above it in one corner is a Muslim mosque.

Centuries ago, after the Arab invasion of Egypt, a village was built within the temple walls. When its mud-brick houses collapsed another one was put on top of it. As this in turned crumbled away, yet more houses were erected on the rubble. Through the years the temple gradually vanished from sight and, during the fourteenth century, a mosque built by a religious man named Abu Hagag was actually high above the site of the great courtyard of Ramses II. It has always been revered because Abu Hagag was a descendant of a saint who lived in Mecca during the lifetime of Muhammad. When the temple was excavated the villagers were rehabilitated outside its walls but the mosque was left where it was.

Luxor has known many names. In ancient times it was called Wast, meaning Sceptre, symbol of rule and authority. The Greek poet Homer referred to it as the 'City of a Hundred Gates' because of its rich temples and monuments but, to most Greeks, it was known as Thebes. When the Arabs came they were also impressed by the city's grandeur and renamed it Al Kasr (castle), which eventually became corrupted into Luxor. It is on the west bank of the Nile, 415 miles (670 km) south of Cairo. EgyptAir has several flights a day from the capital, the airport being about 5 miles north of the town. From there you are taken by taxi or bus along a metalled road to your hotel or steamer through countryside bordered by canals. Should you arrive by train, you can travel by day or in a sleeper at night. If you arrive on a steamer, some of Luxor's hotels can be reached just by walking across the corniche from the jetty. The Old Winter Palace with its semi-circular entrance staircase was beloved by Victorians. Its beautiful garden at the back has morning glories twirling up acacias and sycamores. Rustic benches are placed invitingly facing flower beds and paths. In recent years an Olympic-size swimming pool has been added at the far end of the garden. Between the old hotel and Luxor temple the New Winter Palace was built fairly recently and both are linked by a hallway. From

Luxor temple. Note the mosque in the background

some of the rooms in the newer hotel, you can get a magical night time view of
the temple when it is illuminated.

Several hotels and some shops and cafés are spread along the corniche facing
the Nile, among them the Etap, the Savoy and the Luxor. North of the Etap
you will find the recently opened Luxor Museum and at one of the nearby
landing stages. Dr Ragab has another houseboat where you can buy his famous
papyri. Buses and taxis ply along the corniche but the preferred mode of travel
is surely the gharry with the fringe on top.

Luxor Temple

From the Tenth to the Twenty-fifth Dynasty, the two temples of Luxor and Karnak were the focus of power in Egypt. The pharaohs gave their artists and architects full rein, and riches were lavished on both these great monuments. Amenophis III spent much of his wealth not on wars and conquests but, during the thirty-five years of his reign, on building and embellishing the temples where the tops of obelisks glittered with gold. Known as 'The Magnificent' he approved designs for a hypostyle hall–one where the roof is held up by pillars or columns.

Egyptian monuments of this gigantic size were enlarged by succeeding kings so that in reality a temple was a series of temples. Ramses II's two reigns later added the pylon. Before going into the temple you must examine the vast facade. Carved across it is a lively history of the battle of Kadesh where Ramses won a victory over the Hittites in Lebanon in 1300 B.C. A gargantuan statue of the Pharaoh made from a single block of stone, faces you in front of the pylon (at one time there were six). On the other side stands an obelisk whose fellow was sent to Paris in 1833.

When you walk through the pylon opening, if you look upwards you can see a carving of the wings of Horus overhead which is often found on pylons. Another repetitive feature is the provision of sockets at the top where flagpoles could be placed to fly pennants on festive occasions. You feel dwarfed as you enter the first open colonnaded courtyard: eleven red granite statues of Ramses confront you between the tall pillars which surround it. Do not be surprised if you hear chanting while you walk around because it may be the time for prayer and a muezzin will be calling the faithful from the mosque of Abu Hagag. Each effigy of the Pharaoh has clenched hands and one foot forward as if to walk towards you. They are naked save for a pleated skirt.

One hall is devoted completely to Amenophis' claim to divinity. This insistence may well have been because his mother, although a foreign princess, was not of the royal blood of Egypt. It was the first time so-called tainted blood had mingled with that of the pharaohs. Amenophis asserts in these reliefs that Amen bade Khnum fashion Amenophis' body upon his sacred potter's wheel. Amen tells Mutemua (Amenophis' mother) he has taken the form of her husband and that he is the father of the new child who will become Pharaoh. Isis is close by to breathe life into the new infant. The birth of Amenophis is then depicted in the presence of Thoueris, Goddess of Children, and Bes the god who vanquished evil spirits. The child is suckled by Hathor. The Niles of the north and south purify the child. Horus presents him to Amen. Finally in the last relief, Amenophis sits on the throne of Egypt. The temple's main court is along a magnificent colonnade of seven pairs of gigantic pillars, the famous Hall of Columns. They rise 42 feet (13 m) into the air, topped with papyrus blossoms whose filaments flatten out at the summits to support the architrave, placed horizontally from pillar to pillar. The

Dancing girls about to somersault depicted on a frieze at Luxor temple

columns soar heavenward like two lines of giant redwood trees but instead of the darkness beneath interwoven branches, sunlight streams down their sides and casts shadows over the stone floor like lengths of black carpeting.

The main court of Amenophis III covers a vast area and is surrounded by double aisles of columns in the form of bunches of tied papyrus. The reliefs are well defined. You continue through a maze of chambers and see where the temple has been torn down in places, changed and rebuilt. In one court, Alexander the Great ordered that four columns be dismantled and replaced by a square mass of masonry which was then carved with frescoes. One shows the God of Fertility receiving wine.

During the fourth century, Christians turned part of the temple into a church and you can see religious pictures painted over Pharaonic reliefs. Many of the murals show the splendour of the processions which took place along the paved avenue of ram-headed sphinxes between Luxor and Karnak. The Pharaoh is shown distributing figs, dates, pomegranates and other fruits to the people on the way. Most delightful is a line of dancing girls about to

Luxor temple

Avenue of ram-headed sphinxes at Karnak

somersault in honour of the King. Each girl is bent backwards as far as the knees of the girl behind her with such elasticity that you wonder why they do not actually perform. There are acrobats, musicians are playing and the whole populace is merry, for it is festival time when Pharaoh munificently bestows favours on his people, happy in the knowledge that he is at one with Amen-Ra.

The avenue of ram-headed sphinxes, each with a small statue of Amenophis III between its paws and chin, linked the temples of Luxor and Karnak along a paved route about 1½ miles (2 km) long.

Karnak Temple

It is traditional to visit Karnak temple by horse-drawn carriage (gharry) from your ship or hotel along the corniche which takes about half an hour. It is particularly pleasant if you go in the evening to see the son-et-lumière presentation. Your carriage will pick you up again after the performance. Visitors are not only impressed with Karnak's many temples, statues and the sacred lake, but by its immensity, for it covers over 400 acres (162 hectares). It has more than half a dozen pylons (temple gateways); the walls are over 80 feet (24 m) high and sometimes 25 feet (2.5 m) thick at their base. The first pylon, the largest ever built is 370 feet (113 m) wide and one of its towers is 140 feet (43 m) high. You wonder what visitors thought when they saw it at the peak of its glory. Fortunately records have been discovered and excavations and archaeological work continues.

In Pharaonic days during festivals, nobles and their retinues arrived by barge along the river. After dropping their sails at the landing stages, they made their way to Karnak and all eyes were on the splendid temple towering overhead. Pennants flew from the pylons. Carvings brilliantly painted adorned its walls. Steles of lapis lazuli were set on both sides of the foremost pylon. The facade was inlaid with malachite, silver and gold. Amenophis' royal architect, who had the same name as his master, had set up a 70 foot (21.5 m) colossus of the Pharaoh hewn from gritstone. The gates and columns were decorated with metal. Formal gardens fanned out from the walls. Obelisks towered over all. A fabulous sight by day, it must have seemed paradise by moonlight so that, from the river, even the miserable captives and slaves on board the ships forgot their wretchedness when they saw peerless Karnak.

The temple took centuries to complete but tourists owe much of what they see today to Amenophis III. Other contributors were Thothmes III who bestowed riches from seventeen Asian invasions and the great Queen Hatshepsut, one of whose obelisks you can still see. She ordered two obelisks for her father's court. At the base of the one remaining, there is a description of how it was planned. They were to be made of single blocks of stone without seam or join, capped with electrum to catch the earliest rays of the morning sun and reflect it to both banks of the Nile. The remaining one is still the tallest in Egypt. Thothmes III later had an even taller one made for Karnak which probably stood at the extreme east end of the temple. This is now in the piazza of St John Lateran in Rome and is believed to be the highest in the world.

It is almost impossible to see Karnak in a day. It is so large you can tire easily even while enjoying it. Perhaps the best idea is to go twice, once in the morning or afternoon and then return at night for the son-et-lumière. The latter really gives you an overall picture because of the commentary but in the sunlight you see the details of the marvellous carvings better. Your guide will choose a shady place, perhaps under a column, to tell you about the various halls and chambers.

The magnificent hypostyle hall is the most famous ever built. The roof was supported on 134 columns, many 70 feet (21.5 m) high and 20 feet (6 m) in circumference. All were covered with decorations and inscriptions in vivid colouring; the sun shone through stone fretted openings high in the nave on either side. Beyond this gigantic hall, you come upon the remaining obelisk of Queen Hatshepsut. In the sunlight you can catch glimpses of inlay work at the top.

In one of the open courts built by Ramses III, there is the usual full array of statues that one associates with this Pharaoh but the figures mingle with the columns in a different guise. Although representations of Ramses, they are in mummy raiment symbolic of Osiris. Hands holding the sceptre and whip are crossed outside funerary linen. Despite the fact that the statues are open to the sky, that tourists come and go, cameras click and birds twitter in the crevices, the figures create an atmosphere of great solemnity. Many of the reliefs are complete and as strikingly beautiful as when they were first finished. One which gives particular pleasure is of Ramses offering sacrifices to Amen. Beneath the Pharaoh are seven quite perfectly carved unguent jars, rounded and shaped, so real you would not be surprised if the air was suddenly laden with a sweet fragrance. Each jar represents seven years of the Pharaoh's reign.

One of the most delightful places is a small rectangular chamber which contains two god statues, a male and a female. They are most graceful and were presented to the temple by King Tutankhamun, the only trace of his benificence to be found there. Next to this chamber is an alcove where a plinth holds the granite feet and ankles of one of the colossal statues of Ramses III. If you touch one great foot and draw your fingers across the instep you can actually feel the slender tendons represented in the stone.

In one of the three halls of Seti stands a figure of Ramses II, enormous and mutilated yet splendid. Much is missing–archaeologists work at the jigsaw puzzle of piecing together broken masonry, year after year. The fragments lying around today will become fewer as they resume their rightful places. The very foundations are complex, having been sunk in different ways during various reigns. Salts in the soil and the varying levels of the Nile from year to year have caused damage. Perhaps most thought-provoking is the sacred lake which is artificial and was created during the reign of Thothmes III. Its level varies as in a nilometer due to infiltration from the river. The water appears fathomless, though in fact it is not very deep. Feint white lines of brine at the edge of the stone quay betray the presence of salt. On a square plinth at one corner of the lake crouches a red granite scarab guarding the sacred stretch of water. During the migratory season, the lake is covered by birds of all kinds. Probably wildfowl were netted from these very waters during the Pharaonic times, for cages of wild birds were one of the most impressive gifts to be offered to the gods. During the day you can go down steps at the little quay,

Carved columns in the Hypostyle Hall, Karnak temple

the same ones which the priests descended when they reverently lowered royal cedar barges into the water bearing the bodies of dead pharaohs. These barges encircled the lake seven times before being lifted out and taken to the valley of the Kings. If you dip your fingers in the water you will find it still and warm. Nothing brings back the atmosphere of ancient Thebes better than the son-et-lumière presentation. Strings of horse-drawn carriages make their way along the corniche towards the temple, tourists' voices mingling with the click-clack of hooves. The drivers decant you and patiently await your return chatting together in groups. It is useful to carry a torch for walking round the the temple if it is a moonless night, as the stone flooring is sometimes uneven. The sand is often comfortably warm from the day's sun–but remember that a jacket or jersey is useful as the temperature drops sharply after dark.

You walk along between the ram-headed sphinxes to the pylon entrance. Lights between their paws illuminate the small statues of pharaohs under their chins. Behind them leafy shrubs catch the light. Once inside the first courtyard, floodlights bring the pillar carvings to life and the commentary begins, interspersed with music. You continue walking, stopping to listen at various places until you come to the sacred lake. Behind it are tiers of seats where you sit for the last part of the performance. The water is now illuminated and you can imagine how the small barges were floated across it symbolizing the Sun-God Amen-Ra sailing across the sky by day. Finally the lights dim, the voices and music die away and people begin to leave. Only the granite scarab remains to resume his silent vigil. Gradually your eyes get accustomed to the darkness as you return to your gharry. Still under the spell of ancient Thebes, you drive back to your ship as travellers have done down the ages to sit on deck and watch the stars reflected in the ancient Nile. If you wish to extend the magic of the evening and are staying at the Movenpick hotel, your carriage will drive you the extra $2\frac{1}{2}$ miles beyond Luxor.

This hotel belonging to the well-known Swiss chain, is on Crocodile Island in the river. Close to the shore, it is reached over a causeway. It is a hotel village with bungalows set among palm trees and lush greenery with views over the Nile. It has a jogging track and, amongst other activities, it offers felucca trips, camel riding, water polo, desert excursions and a swimming pool. Beyond the Crocodile Bar in the lobby is a gourmet restaurant which is one of the best in Upper Egypt and features Swiss specialities. The Fellah's Tent is an alternative restaurant where you can choose from an oriental buffet. The freshly baked 'baladi' bread is delicious with mashi, shish kebab kufta and tahina, but you can read more about Egyptian fare in the chapter on food and drink. Here you will be able to watch local villagers give folkloric displays including the stick dance when men swing sticks over their heads and stage a mock battle. Of course there is belly-dancing and oriental music. If you want something more relaxing there is always the Sunset Arena where you can listen to classical music.

Shopping is well worthwhile in Luxor where galabiehs can be made within a day and alabaster ornaments are less expensive than in other places as the quarries are nearby. Alabaster has been extensively worked in Egypt since ancient times when it was used for unguent and perfume jars, statues and ornaments. Today hollow vases and table lamps can be internally lit which shows the veining to perfection. It varies in colour from deep amber to pale honey, sometimes intermingled with white. The only trouble for tourists is that it is heavy for air baggage. Fortunately you can buy small things such as pyramids, ashtrays and other carvings.

Scarabs–which are amulets made in the form of a beetle–are unusual and interesting things to buy. They are small to carry and may cost quite a lot or be very cheap. They were regarded by the ancient Egyptians as a sign or immortality on a mummy to guard it in the interval between death and life in the hereafter. The female beetle rolls a speck of cow dung into a ball and burrows into the earth with it, remaining quiescent for some months before emerging again. During the hibernation, she lays an egg in the dung and this now hatches out. So life issues again from darkness.

You can buy scarabs in all sizes from half an inch up to five inches or more, made of various materials from clay to stone. Antique scarabs are generally turquoise in colour, varying from a bright hue to one scarcely discernible. It is difficult even for experts to tell the ancient from the modern, but if you find one which pleases you what does it matter whether it was made yesterday or 500 years ago? I love one merchant's reply when asked if a scarab was genuine. 'Of course it is. I made it myself this morning in my kitchen!' The variety is amazing and the inscriptions on the back differ considerably. Some are even made in semi-precious stones such as amber, cornelian or zircon but they are difficult to find. Onnig, my jeweller in Cairo, has made a few in slate as pendants but they are awkward to produce as slate is fragile and cracks easily.

Most of the hotels along the corniche have shopping areas in their lobbies and there is a maze of small shops next to the New Winter Palace. As has been mentioned before, beyond the Etap there is a small museum which you should not miss.

The Luxor Museum

Quite apart from the exhibits this is a very modern and unusual museum. You walk up a few steps and enter an air-conditioned, dimly-lit hall where the antiquities are in illuminated glass cabinets so that every detail can be seen. Only large items like statues and sections of wall are not encased but all are well lit.

The first cabinet you see, number 196, contains a tranquil head of a cow covered in gold, the large eyes outlined in black. It is from the tomb of Tutankhamun and represents the goddess Mehit Werit who welcomed the King into the world of the dead. There is a bust of Amenhotep III wearing the double crown of Egypt. It once belonged to a huge statue which decorated a funerary temple in Western Thebes. Another head of the same king wearing the double crown is also on display, which once belonged to a seated statue in

In a parade at Luxor, animals are dressed up too. This camel sports a kerchief and some old light bulbs

Karnak. A tall figure of the god Sobek, a man's body with a crocodile's head, looms protectively over yet another representation of Amenhotep III, the detail and perfect balance between the god and the king making the tableau a work of art. Exhibit number 110 is of Sekmet, lioness God of War. She once stood in the temple of Mut at Karnak.

Glass cabinets and statues line the hall, each so interesting that you are suddenly at the far end of the hall without realizing it. Here you come to a semi-circular ramp to your right. Walking up this and turning right again, you pass back down the hall with exhibits on either side. Huge slabs of limestone wall from the temples of Karnak and Luxor are displayed on the left, lit in such a way that the grooves which make up the pictures give life to them. One depicts Akhnaton and Nefertiti worshipping the Sun Disc; another is from the temple of Amenhotep IV at Karnak. More cabinets cointain jewelry and other artifacts. Number 200 holds two small funerary boats from Tutankhamun's tomb. They are replicas of those which bore his mummified body and Ka (soul) to Abydos and back to make contact with Osiris before returning to his tomb in the Valley of the Kings. Number 206 is a tiny alabaster crocodile, so realistic that it could be a yellow baby reptile. At the end a shallow ramp leads down to the steps by which you entered the building. The museum opens about 5.00 pm but times alter according to season. Check with your ship or hotel.

8

THE VALLEYS OF THE
KINGS AND QUEENS
AND THE
NECROPOLIS of THEBES

It is the Nile more than anything else which will remain in your mind after a visit to Egypt. From its source in the heights of Eritrea, it flows through the Sudan and Egypt giving life to both and then floods into the Mediterranean. Nowhere is it more dramatic than at Luxor where in ancient times it divided the living on one side from the dead on the other; the town on the east bank and probably the most elaborate necropolis in the world on the west bank of the river.

It is important to visit the Luxor and Karnak temples before crossing the Nile so that you can comprehend the fixation which the Pharaonic era had with death. As soon as a king mounted the throne his first priority was to arrange a suitable tomb for his eventual demise. Queens and nobles did the same and further down the scale the custom was carried on according to one's means and station in life. The concern over a suitable burial place was only exceeded by the need to preserve the body. The soul or Ka, being divine, could somehow flit through life to eternity but it seemed essential to preserve one's physical form. Thus the art of mummification came to the fore, taking many years to reach ultimate perfection. This macabre practice was begun some thousands of years before the birth of Christ and had to avoid disfiguration of any kind.

Only special guilds were permitted to undertake the preservation of human bodies after death. It was done in three different ways. The most skilful and therefore most expensive method was by extracting the brain through the nose with specially designed instruments without altering the facial expression in any way. Intestines were removed through the side with a sharp thin blade. The cavities were then filled with myrrh, cassia and other fragrant herbs, the hole sewn up and the body immersed in natron (sesquicarbonate of soda) for 70 days. After being washed it was finally wrapped in strips of fine linen and smeared with gum. According to one authority, this cost a talent of silver, the equivalent of more than 1000 Egyptian pounds today. The second alternative was far less complicated. The entrails were dissolved, the brain was not removed but the body was again put into natron for 70 days. This procedure was half the price of the first and dispersed all save skin and bones. The third way was most commonly used as it was cheaper and consisted of injecting a strong astringent into the body, followed by the usual pickling in natron.

In the first method, the organs were mummified separately by washing in palm oil and powdering with aromatic herbs after which they were sealed in four jars. One held the heart and the others the liver and two intestines. The jars were made of alabaster or terracotta and each was inscribed. The god to whom each was dedicated protected it. The jars were buried with the mummy together with small ushabti figures, glazed faience statuettes, who would assist the mummy in the underworld. Amulets were placed around the neck of the dead, amongst them the papyrus sceptre, emblem of the youth hoped for in the next world; the vulture ensuring the protection of Isis; the buckle, a small red stone symbolic of the blood of Isis; the key of life and the utchat in the form of an eye, the sign of good health and happiness. Other sacred things protected the body including scarabs and modelled index and middle fingers representing the two fingers of Horus stretched out to aid the dead. As soon as a man died he became identified with Osiris, for it was supposed that this god had been the first to be embalmed, and that Anubis the jackal-headed god had been the chief embalmer.

Professor Bryan Emery relates in his book *Archaic Egypt* that mummies of the Second Dynasty had an almost human appearance. 'The features of the deceased are modelled in detail as are the genitals and, in the case of women, the breasts and nipples.'

It was believed that the dead traversed a long lonely river called the Tuat before attaining the glory of Ra. The Tuat, which was neither above nor below the level of Egypt, had its source on the west bank of the Nile, ran north, then curved round to the east and ended where the sun rose. It was divided into twelve parts beginning and ending with a chamber. The entrance was called Amentet, a place of twilight. As the deceased continued the awful journey the darkness became complete. Horrible monsters and hideous reptiles would rise from the depths of boiling water. These had to be overcome with help from the gods. In the final section the way gradually lightened until the last chamber where the glory of Ra was revealed.

The priests taught the faithful the various divisions of the Tuat, and where the worst dangers threatened, with the aid of pictures and knowledge gleaned from the *Book of the Dead*. They presided over the construction of royal tombs and saw to it that the subterranean passages joining the chambers and halls resembled the long narrow valley of death.

Burial services were symbolic of the after-life. The body was laid on a boat in the funeral procession on a carriage drawn by oxen. Priests burned incense and chanted. Mourners wearing grey-blue robes wailed. They were followed by servants and slaves carrying furniture, chests of jewelry, chariots, food and all the impedimenta that was to be buried with the deceased. At the tomb dancers and musicians awaited the mummy which on arrival was placed upright for the ceremony called the 'Opening of the Mouth'. Very little is

Colossi of Memnon, Luxor

known of this save that the priests intoned formulae and offerings were held before the body which was put in its final resting place. The priests emerged from the vaults chanting sacred words. All had been accomplished that would ensure safety for the mummy. Before resurrection it rested among the treasures acquired during lifetime. The Ka was thought to pass from the mummy to the gods and return again. It could eat, drink and find pleasure, a personality without form although it is depicted as a human-headed bird. To ensure that nothing should be touched or stolen by human hands, the burial chambers had to be hidden deep underground.

Ferried across the Nile to the west bank, you used to be greeted by strings of donkeys but today, after scaling a flight of steps, you will find buses and taxis waiting to take you to the sites. Most tours start either early in the morning or at about 4.00 pm to avoid the heat of the day. This is particularly pleasant in the spring and summer when dawn is breaking and the Nile reflects the rising sun and wispy clouds ranging in colour from faint pink to purple. Considering that there are now hundreds of tourists of many nationalities, the tour operators are quite successful in dovetailing the visits to tombs so that waiting is minimized. The temples, being large, do not present the same problem as they can accommodate several parties at once and you can often overhear commentaries in different languages.

You drive along a tree-lined road between fields of sugar cane and irrigation canals and in a short time see the Colossi of Memnon in the distance. Due to the clear air distances are deceptive. When you leave your vehicle and walk towards them they seem very close. It is only when you notice the tiny figures of other tourists moving around their base that you realize how big they are. They stand a good 60 feet (18 m) tall. They were once in front of a vast funerary temple belonging to Amenophis III which vanished long ago so completely that it is thought there may have been an earthquake. They face the rising sun each dawn and around their large feet the Nile in flood used to lap before the dams decreed otherwise. They have been photographed nearly as often as the Sphinx and travellers in the past have inscribed the bases with signatures in different languages.

The Colossi were given their name by early Greek travellers when it was rumoured that they represented the Trojan hero Memnon. According to one, Petronianus, they made a wailing sound each morning as the sun rose to its mother Eros at dawn. Roman visitors including the Emperor Hadrian heard the 'vocal Memnon'. As one colossus was fractured the sound may have been caused when the wind blew in a certain direction. Some historians claim it was a priest acting as an oracle. When Septimus Severus had the damaged Colossus repaired, there was no more mention of this almost human sound. The mighty shoulders are 20 feet (6 m) across, the forearms from elbow to finger tip 15 feet (4.5 m) and the fingers over 4 feet (1.2 m) long.

West of the Colossi a short distance away is Ramses III's temple at Medinet Habu.

Medinet Habu

When Thebes first became the capital of Egypt, it was believed that one of the primordial hills of the earth was situated within the precincts of what later became the temple district of Medinet Habu, which includes the Colossi. It was here that Ramses III decided to have his mortuary temple and it was to be built in his own lifetime. He succeeded in this but, due to the haste, the workmanship is not as consistent as in his father's (Ramses II) temples, nor does it have the delicacy of carving that his grandfather (Seti I) achieved at Abydos. The lines are bold, the inscriptions deeply cut. If you put your hand in one of them it will vanish up to the wrist.

Ramses III copied his father in many ways. His children were given the same names, he had a pet lion trained to race alongside his chariot and commissioned reliefs depicting his victories in battle. On the second pylon he is shown parading captives before the gods Amun and Mut while on the other he triumphs over the Syrians who invaded Egypt during his reign. He bestowed wealth on his temple during his lifetime–as is evidenced by the lists carved on the wall–and many feasts were held. Two offertory chambers have waist-high shelves where fruit, flowers, food, wine and perfumes were placed. One of the largest outside walls shows Ramses hunting large bulls. Another shows him born on a litter preceded by priests during a festival. The Queen accompanies the Pharaoh and the royal couple are surrounded by fan bearers and attendants. No corner of the temple seems to be without a montage of daily royal life. In yet another the King is presenting offerings to Min, the god of fertility. Scenes of the aftermath of war are cruel. Ramses is shown meting out justice from his chariot to groups of miserable captives. They are to have their genitals and right hands cut off at the wrist. Pharaoh–in his magnaminity–allows the prisoners a feast before the punishment. A naval battle is in progress in a war scene where a ship has been damaged and victims are in the water. A humane touch shows Egyptian sailors swimming to help the drowning. The real delight of this temple is the colouring in which inner walls and ceilings look as if they were painted yesterday. Though open to the sky and searing sunlight, cameos and decorations have survived amazingly well. One wonders how the colours were mixed to achieve this miracle. Two ceilings are especially beautiful with the cool blue-green of turquoise predominating. An amusing plump water bird struts along one segment, its feathers red, blue and white, its beak a shiny hydrangea blue!

The Ramesseum

The Ramesseum, mortuary temple of Ramses II, is about $\frac{2}{3}$ mile or 1 km from Medinet Habu. Although partly in ruins it is impressive. You enter it through the second court past four seated granite statues of the Pharaoh. Then you see the enormous statue of Ramses lying on the ground broken into three pieces. Made from a single granite block, it weighed over 1000 tons (1016 tonnes).

Although a seated figure it was 56 feet (17 m) high. The upper arms are inscribed with Ramses' name in hieroglyphics. The story goes that the Persian King Cambyses ordered the statue to be broken. Shelley describes the shattered image thus:

> Two vast and trunkless legs of stone
> Stand in the desert...Near them, on the sand,
> Half sunk, a shattered visage lies, whose frown,
> And wrinkled lip, and sneer of cold command,
> Tell that it's sculptor well those passions read

Although the temple is in such a state of disrepair you can see it is similar to Karnak but on a smaller scale. Building was a passion with Ramses and he knew he could not reproduce the immensity of Karnak, which after all had taken hundreds of years to construct. He determined, like Ramses III after him, to finish his masterpiece during his lifetime and to make up in its decoration what it lacked in size. In this he was successful as can be seen in the vivid reliefs of his triumph at Kadesh.

Along the length of the hypostyle hall were eight rows of columns resembling (but not as grandiose as) those at Karnak. Some were 36 feet (10 m) tall and their lotus bud capitals are so finely worked that, where they are still standing, they appear to cling to the roof rather than support it.

Ramses wished to record for posterity his greatest victory, that at Kadesh, now part of Lebanon. The story has also been chronicled in the temples of Luxor, Abu Simbel and Abydos but nowhere in such lively fashion as in the Ramesseum. In Lebanon this victory started a trend which has been followed there ever since. He had the story inscribed in hieroglyphics on the first of a series of flat cliff faces along the dog river-called the Orontes in his day.The Dog River, Nahr el Kelb, is just on the outskirts of Beirut and you can still see today a series of steles cut in the cliff face. Others have been added since in different languages, some later defaced by succeeding conquerors. Among contributors are Nebuchadnezzar, Napoleon and the French General Gouraud who proclaimed the Lebanese Republic in 1920. While on this Lebanese diversion it is interesting to note that, as Julian Huxley speculates in his book *From an Antique Land,* there must have been a connection between the Dog River and the Egyptian Jackal-God Anubis.

To return to the Kadesh battle. According to the accounts on the temple walls it seems to have happened in this way. The Hittites had been making nuisances of themselves by skirmishing along the border. Ramses decided he had had enough and would stop further trouble by inflicting a major defeat. In 1288 B.C. he marched his troops through Palestine to the border with Lebanon, his confidence growing as he advanced. At dawn one morning, leaving his main force behind, he forded the Orontes River with a detachment to seek out the enemy camp but found nothing. Two bedouin were asked if they had any information and reported that Metella, the Hittite king, had fled to the north with his followers. Delighted with this news Ramses continued north unaware that Metella had paid the bedouin to tell him the story. As Ramses advanced, Metella closed in behind him. Towards the end of the day, the Pharaoh made preparations to bivouac near the river for the night. Suddenly, some of his soldiers took prisoner a couple of Asiatics and brought them before the Pharaoh. When questioned, they said that the Egyptians were being followed and even as they were speaking the Hittites struck.

Ramses was furious. He mounted his war chariot and, with his men around him and his pet lion running beside him, turned on the enemy. At one time in the ensuing fight he was alone but, such was his fury he managed to throw several of his enemies into the river. Fortunately, the main body of his army—having presumably heard the uproar—arrived and joined in the battle, turning the tide in the Egyptians' favour.

The Hittites had by now formed up on the opposite bank of the narrow Orontes and were pulling survivors from the water. One splendid relief shows the Sultan of Aleppo being inverted to drain the water out of him! Metella was amazed to see his own brother and attendant scribe being pitched into the river. By dusk it was all over and Ramses had achieved the victory he wanted but he proved to be a generous adversary. Some fifteen years later he married King Metella's eldest daughter, thus consolidating peaceful relations between the warring factions. He bestowed the name Matnefrure on her, meaning 'Who sees the beauty of Ra'.

After this, Ramses prowess was envied throughout Asia where the belief grew that he was surely begotten of their War Goddess Anat. This notoriety pleased him and he renamed his favourite daughter Anat.

You pass the valley of the Queens on the way to Hatshepsut's great temple. It is estimated that there are more than fifty tombs there but not many open. Two or three are well worth visiting but the limestone in this area does not lend itself to the cutting of reliefs so the scenes are painted.Those that you can visit are not deep and you can walk straight into them as if entering a cave. There are railings and illumination so that you can admire the scenes of rural life with animals, trees, flowers and vines. Here there are not so many royal trappings. The Valley of the Nobles and Priests is livelier and tomb 52, that of Nakht, scribe of granaries, has the famous coloured frieze of dancing girls, reproduced so much as decoration for tapestries and bags. The bright colouring and general air of cheerfulness make them well worth visiting. If time is short, even a few minutes in one will give you an idea of what the others contain. Just before reaching Deir el Bahri where you visit Queen Hatshepsut's temple, you will see the old rest house of Thomas Cook, on a small hill. He was the first travel agent to bring a party of tourists to this extraordinary place over a century ago.

Queen Hatshepsut's Temple

One of the mightiest and wealthiest queens of all time, Hatshepsut had the power to choose any place she wished for her own special temple and she

Queen Hatshepsut's temple near the Valley of Kings

picked a splendid site in Deir el Bahri. You cannot but be impressed when you first see it. Divided from the Valley of the Kings by a spectacular bare ridge of cinnamon-coloured cliffs, it presents a dramatic picture. To select it as the site for a temple to outshine all others was pure genius.

Hatshepsut's family tree is so interwoven and her own marriages so confusing and incestuous, that even genealogists find it bewildering. It runs something like this. She was daughter of Thothmes I and his half sister Aahmes. Her father's second wife, Mut Nefert, bore a son who became Thothmes II. He married Hatshepsut, his half-sister. Thothmes II married a second wife, a woman of low rank, who bore him an heir. So it came about that Hatshepsut was both half-sister and wife of Thothmes II and was made guardian of her stepson and nephew who became Thothmes III.

Indulged by her father throughout her teens, Hatshepsut became ambitious and autocratic. After her father's death when her half-brother/husband

Thothmes II ascended the throne, she gradually took over affairs of state as her husband hated court life and preferred leading his army against raiding tribes on his borders. He also discovered as pharaohs before him had done, that winning battle could bring great rewards. Little by little, Hatshepsut took over the running of the country which she enjoyed and the Pharaoh hated. She was aided and advised by a brilliant scribe who rose from obscurity and was eventually to become the highest in the land after the great Queen herself. His name was Setmut and, among his many accomplishments, he must have been a clever architect for he is thought to have designed Hatshepsut's magnificent temple. Certainly it is inscribed that he 'executed the eternal monuments' of the Queen.

Deir el Bahri was intended to be a mortuary temple and Hatshepsut's burial vault was constructed beneath it, but she was eventually buried in the Valley of the Kings. No doubt this would have pleased her even more as, during her lifetime, she adopted the style of a pharaoh, even in encouraging military power. Her body has never been found.

Thothmes survived his campaigns to die of natural causes while still a young man. Hatshepsut's nephew Thothmes III was still a child so it was natural for the Queen to act as regent. However, she wished to rule exclusively and take over the late Pharaoh's role, even to the insignia and ritual false beard. (Pharaohs always kept themselves hairless and the royal beards were false). As the young prince grew up he became more like his father. He hated court life and wished to be a warrior and lead armies on the battlefield. Hatshepsut refused to let him go, fearing he might be killed and threaten her royal lifestyle. He was made to take part in processions and festivals and came to dislike Hatshepsut. At her command he married her daughter but, as he grew to manhood, his dislike turned to hatred. When she died he had as many of her monuments, reliefs and cartouches destroyed as he could. Fortunately for us he did not entirely succeed.

Hatshepsut's temple, although inland and beyond the line of green cultivation, faces the Nile. From its entrance you can get a wonderful view back over the river. It is constructed on a plan unique in Egypt. Parts are cut into the living rock of the cliff face and the remainder, made of local stone, combines into an edifice the like of which you will not find anywhere else. You approach it, not through the usual pylon but along a wide ramp. Large porticos with colonnades lead off either side of this processional ramp in three tiers. A lion once stood on either side at the beginning of the ramp leading to the second terrace, which housed the Holy of Holies and other chambers.

The reliefs on the walls of the first colonnade display various highlights of the Queen's life. One shows the two obelisks from the granite quarries of Aswan for Karnak temple in honour of her father. They are placed base to base on a raft which is taking them northward to Luxor. It is towed by three ships manned by scores of oarsmen. You can still see one of these obelisks in its rightful place at Karnak, the other has disappeared.

Pictures in the hall on the left side of the ground level terrace, trace the story of an expedition sent by the Queen to Punt on the Red Sea. This was to obtain myrrh trees to be planted in her temple. The expedition is seen setting off with merchandise to barter and a large statue of the Queen as a gift. Her men were greeted by the Prince of Punt and his family. Unlike the attractive figures of the rest of the Prince's retinue, his wife, in a yellow robe, is shown as extremely fat. As royal figures were always carved as slender and attractive, some Egyptologists think that the lady may have been suffering from elephantiasis.

The scenes at Punt are interesting. Domestic animals wander among huts and cows browse beneath shady trees. Frescoes show Hatshepsut's men loading up their ships for the voyage home. The myrrh trees are planted in urns to survive the journey back to Egypt, each carried aboard by six men using ropes slung over their shoulders. Heavily laden with gifts and bartered goods, the ships lie deep in the water. Men continue to clamber up gang planks carrying sacks. Baboons scamper on the cargo. Artistic licence portrays fish in the water of exaggerated size not found in the Nile. These salt water fish include sharks, giant rays, swordfish and even whales. The frieze story ends happily as the ships return to Egypt. Hatshepsut is content and the myrrh trees flourish and decorate her temple gardens. There are two footnotes to the tale. Part of the reliefs were cut from the wall at one time but have been replaced. In recent years fossilized myrrh trees have been found in excavations.

In the hall and chambers on the right of the ground level terrace, Hatshepsut, like many other Egyptian rulers, claims divine birth in a series of reliefs. Several propound the idea that she was begotten of a god. The Queen Mother is shown being told by Amun that Hatshepsut's birth is the result of divine intervention. 'Hatshepsut shall be the name of thy daughter. She shall exercise kingship in this whole land.' Gods are depicted bringing gifts for the child. Later she reappears as a young girl in the presence of Amun and he puts his hand on her shoulder protectively. In an antechamber, she can be seen on her knees being suckled by Hathor, the Cow Goddess, the head held at a queenly angle.

Although it is obvious from numerous shattered and blank walls that Thothmes III succeeded in having many of the Queen's pictures removed, in some instances the vandalism only partially worked. Through erasures, rich reliefs still show with astonishing persistence. During Hatshepsut's reign, building reached great artistic heights as can be judged by her handsome temple. War was discouraged and trade flourished. Although ruthless in many ways her beauty, iron will and foresight proved to many of her subjects that, to a queen who was divine, nothing was impossible.

At the entrance to the temple, as with many others you will find enterprising vendors doing their best to sell you souvenirs, some useful and attractive, some rubbish. Bargaining is the order of the day if you see anything you want, and it is all conducted in a light-hearted vein. You will be offered alabaster ornaments, scarves, hats, jewelry, but remember you have got to carry it home if you buy it. I saw a girl outside the temple one morning early, pondering whether to buy a charming little replica of the famous Nefertiti head. 'It is the only one of its kind here today lady' said the merchant. 'Why, there is a smaller one over there on the sand' she said indignantly. The man smiled. 'Ah lady, that is not Nefertiti. It is her daughter!' Another visitor was considering a scribe's head and shoulders and asked if it was genuine. 'Of course, Sir. Look at the back.' The man did so. Printed on it was 'Made in Hong Kong'.

The collecting of antiques has always been popular in Egypt, but since the opening of Tutankhamun's tomb, it has increased and visitors still hope to find something genuine or unusual. It is natural for the fellaheen to scan their fields and the desert because things are often unearthed, especially in places like the Valley of the Kings. One Luxor merchant in Victorian times was reputed to have made a fortune by, amongst other things, offering a new skull cap to any fellah who brought one to him full of scarabs. It may have happened then but not today.

Driving from Hatshepsut's temple to the Valley of the Kings, you pass by some old houses once owned by such people as Howard Carter, between the wars. Today a few have been refurbished by other Egyptologists working among the monuments. They are of several different nationalities and are steadily excavating and restoring tombs and temples. A Polish team have done a lot of repair and reconstruction on Hatshepsut's temple.

There is a small alabaster factory nearby where taxis and buses stop for tourists. It is difficult to leave once you enter for there is an alabaster quarry close by and they have some lovely things at reasonable prices. Shelves contain vases of all sizes, bowls, small pyramids and ashtrays in honey colours from deep amber to pale yellow and beige. Some items are polished and gleaming while others have a rough finish–but there are light bulbs on the shelves so that you can hold anything up and examine the translucent veining. Bargaining is brisk and tends to continue until you return to your vehicle.

Tombs in the Valley of the Kings

We tend to associate the word valley with water and greenery but this one is dry and sandy, its bare hillsides sheer and fissured by searing heat and wind. At midday the sunlight turns the cliffs yellow against a vivid blue sky and the heat can be uncomfortable. Dawn and late afternoon are the times to come to this strange place. The colours are softer, there is often a breeze and the tombs are cool. The Rest House, the only modern building, is air-conditioned and somehow manages to fit into the sparse landscape. Buses park a little away from the area so there are no traffic problems. In some ways it is a sombre place. After all it is a cemetery, but tourists do not seem out of place and the scale is large enough to dwarf curious sightseers. The number of people allowed in any one tomb at a time is controlled. The claustrophobic should think twice before entering some of the deeper tombs. In the Rest House you can order cooling drinks, coffee, tea or snacks. There are also washrooms and, if you are female, do not be surprised to be offered towels by a man in the ladies room because this is the custom.

The tombs are numbered and each has a notice outside to tell you about the person whose grave it is or was. Thothmes I was the first Pharaoh to break away from the pyramid as a burial place. Knowing how such graves had been plundered despite every precaution thought up by priests, it was felt that it might be wiser to hide the actual grave as well as the Pharaoh's body and possessions. This was discussed with the high priests and it was decided that no one would dare desecrate a royal tomb during the priest's lifetime. When they and the architects and workmen who had been concerned with the tomb died, there was more likelihood of the whereabouts being forgotten than if a large monument stood to remind everyone. The cliffs of Thebes were bare; no one visited them for there was nothing to see and nothing grew there. Best of all, because the cliffs were of limestone they reflected the sunlight and remained cool. In addition the stone is soft and therefore easily worked and neither is it porous.

The Theban hills kept their secret well for a time but, as more pharaohs died and were buried there more people knew. Although the priests warned of the horrible afterlife awaiting any who violated them, there were always those who dared risk such hazards when, during their human life, they could have what they desired. So grave robbers flourished. Although many tombs are hidden to this day, sixty-four have already been uncovered but who knows where the fabulous things they contained have gone. At least many of their beautiful decorations have survived and these can be visited today.

The choice is usually made for you by your guide and it is simpler to go along with his selection. If you do have a choice, my favourite ones are Tutankhamun, Seti I, Ramses VI and Amenhotep II. Tutankhamun's tomb seems to be the most popular with visitors, perhaps because they have already seen in museums, things found there by Howard Carter in the 1920s, yet it is quite small.

The tomb entrances usually have wooden banisters either side and down the centre of the flights of steps so that you go down one side and return up the other.

The size of a pharaoh's tomb was governed indirectly by the length of his life. The longer he lived the more treasures he acquired and, as these had to be buried with him, so his grave had to be enlarged to accommodate them. Because Tutankhamun died before he was twenty years old, his is not very deep. Nor is there much wall decoration but when you get to the burial chamber, the paintings are so marvellous and vivid that the figures might be alive.

On the back wall the Pharaoh is seen with his right arm about Osiris' shoulder while his Ka in human form holds him around the waist at the back. On one side wall are twelve squares depicting the twelve months of the year. Symbolic murals cover the opposite one, in the centre of which is the sacred boat of Amen-Ra. Overhead the Goddess of the Soul is shown in the form of a bird, wings spread out protectively, with the Key of Life clasped in its claws.

You can lean over wooden railings to look down at the sarcophagus whose cover has been replaced with glass through which can be seen the largest of the gilded wood mummiform coffins with the actual mummy of the young Pharoah inside it. Originally there were three mummiforn coffins nested within each other, the one which encased the body being of solid gold. The two inner ones have been removed to the Cairo Museum. Imagine what the funeral cortege must have looked like in the Eighteenth Dynasty, comprising not only the mummy with its golden trappings but with all the magnificent worldly treasures carried in procession.

Seti I's tomb was uncovered by an Italian Egyptologist, Giovanni Battista Belzoni. He first went to Egypt in 1812 where he designed a hydraulic machine for raising the water of the Nile. He visited the temples of Edfu and Philae, discovered the temple of Abu Simbel in 1817 and was the first to enter the Second Pyramid. In 1822 he gave exhibitions in Paris and London of facsimiles of Seti I's tomb which caused great interest, especially in London where the exhibition was held in the Egyptian Hall in Piccadilly. The following year he set out for West Africa, hoping to reach Timbuktu but died of dysentery on his way inland from Benin.

Seti's tomb is the deepest burial vault in the world. Two downward flights of steps lead into a long inclined passage which is linked to chambers and halls by further narrow stairways. The walls are covered with pictures of Seti's journey through Tuat accompanied by Amen-Ra. The passages are 500 feet (153 m) long and lead down to a depth of 150 feet (46 m). As was customary, the day Seti died work ceased on his tomb and it is believed many of his retinue, architects and artists were killed and entombed at the same time to ensure secrecy.

Two pillared halls and antechambers lead to the final resting place where the sarcophagus should be. The high vaulting overhead is supported by six pillars cut in the rock. The walls are smooth to the touch and covered with vividly coloured paintings. The ceiling, with authentic starry constellations, is of midnight blue save in the space exactly over the sarcophagus where there is a carved circular zodiac. The River Tuat flows along one wall. Breaking the surface is a fat-bellied crocodile, its jaws wide open, drops of water sliding off its green scales. The Goddess Isis reclines gracefully in a sacred barge. A gigantic scarab clings to the flat surface of the wall, ebony black in colour.

The sarcophagus has gone. Belzoni offered it for sale and eventually it was sold for £2000 to Sir John Soane. It is one of the most beautiful of its kind and is now in the Soane Museum in Lincoln's Inn Fields in London. Made from alabaster it is inscribed with scenes and texts from the 'Book of Gates'. It is sculptured inside and out with hundreds of delicately carved figures each about two inches high.

The tomb of Ramses VI, like Seti I an elderly man, was opened three times. The first time was by grave robbers who not only ransacked it but resealed it afterwards and it was not until the Graeco-Roman period that it was again found. Many travellers of those days visited it as can be seen by their signatures on the walls. The tomb was rediscovered in the Victorian era by a wealthy villager who was interested in archaeology. It shows much ingenuity with its concealed passages leading off at odd angles. The mummy was taken by the original vandals. It would be interesting to know which alabaster jars, perfume bottles, drinking goblets and other objects scattered among the world's museums came from this Pharaoh's tomb.

Ramses VI's tomb was wrongfully supposed by many Greeks to be that of Memnon, probably because of the many Greek inscriptions. The Pharaoh's wealth can be judged by the paintings of many chariots, numerous jars of oil and wine and palace furnishings of all kinds. He is seen making obeisance and presenting offerings to the deities. He is threatened by angy crocodiles and hissing serpents. The dangers of the Tuat seem insurmountable but help is always at hand in the form of special hieroglyphic inscriptions, sacred scarabs and cartouches. At the end of each corridor there is a bend round which sunlight must have been reflected by mirrors to give the artists light for their work. In this sombre place the walls are covered with scenes of life: pictures of slaves and prisoners who took part in its building. Some near the site of the sarcophagus are headless, no doubt *pour encourager les autres*! Some artists are shown painting upside down hanging by their heels in places which they could not reach standing up. Perhaps this helped them to achieve the right perspective!

Ships glide along the ceiling of the innermost hall which is of such porportions that the stone sarcophagus in the centre appears minute. Along one wall gods are shown in a sacred barge using piety instead of radar to avoid a bloated green crocodile which is rising from the blue Tuat. Mammoth snakes coil and twist about the cornice. The vaulting is divided between the Goddess of Life and the Goddess of Death. The wings of Horus spread protectively over all. When it is remembered what fabulous things were discovered in Tutankhamun's small tomb, the mind boggles at the wealth which Ramses' vault must have yielded.

The tomb of Amenhotep II was discovered by an archaeologist of yet another nationality, the Frenchman Victor Loret. In 1899 a wall of stone beyond a sunken well in the cliff face was tested by him and sounded hollow. Excavations were begun and revealed the tomb. A deep shaft nearby had served to conceal it and put would-be marauders off the scent for centuries. The Frenchman was delighted with his find for not only was much treasure discovered but hidden in it were several royal mummies: those of Amenhotep II, Ramses IV, V and VI, Thothmes IV, Amenophis III and Meneptah. The vault had obviously been used as a royal hiding place by the priests for the pharaohs whose tombs had been molested. Many of these mummies are now in the Cairo Museum. The excavations were so meticulously carried out that none of the painted walls or columns has suffered in anyway. Stars shine down from a bright blue stone ceiling. Dressed in transparent linen, life size figures on square pillars in one hall are protected by glass and illuminated. Many are of the gods Hathor and Anubis giving the Key of Life to members of the royal family. The figures of these men and women appear to be alive and about to walk toward you. It is fascinating that both sexes had their finger and toe nails enamelled white.

Before leaving Luxor you must go for a sail in a felucca at sunset. The views on both sides of the river are completely different, one being solitary cliffs round the Valley of the Kings shimmering in the half light from the heat of the day, the other Luxor temple rising above the busy corniche with cruise steamers in the foreground. As the sun sinks lower, fish leap from the river making circles in the water and birds wing back to the trees on shore. The horizon changes from gold to pink as you glide along. Darkness comes and the sail is lowered before docking. There is often an afterglow for a few minutes when the sun finally disappears and the sky is reflected in the water in orange and lilac. It is something not to be missed.

9

THE TEMPLES OF

ESNA, EDFU
AND
KOM OMBO

Esna is about 34 miles (55 km) south of Luxor. Many Copts live there and at one time it was a great monastic centre. Its dam is 2870 feet (874 m) long and has 120 sluice gates. Your ship ties up near the remains of an ancient pier built during the time of the Ptolemies. After climbing up a little bank you reach a pathway beside the river and after some ten minutes walk along it come to the town. The temple is in the middle of Esna which has a population of about 30,000. You are suddenly in a busy street. The frontless shops seem to have more furniture, for which the place is famous, than anything else. Chests of drawers, tables and other things in process of being made spill out over the narrow pavements and there is the pleasant smell of sandalwood. Galabiehs hang above and around shop entrances and if you wish to buy one the merchant will reach it down for you with a bamboo pole. They are popular for tourists because, even if you are only on a five day trip, on one of the nights on board there is almost bound to be a galabieh party when everyone is expected to wear one.

Towards the centre of the town you suddenly come upon railings to one side of the road and when you walk up to them you can look down at the temple some 30 feet (9 m) below, dedicated to the ram-headed God Khnum. The reason that it is below ground level is that it had been completely buried under successive layers of the town built above it over the centuries. When it was rediscovered, major excavation work was necessary to expose it again to public gaze. Indeed this temple was built by the Romans and Ptolomies some two centuries B.C. on top of an even earlier one made by Thothmes III during the Eighteenth dynasty. There is a joke about the people of Esna which relates that they were so used to seeing capitals growing in the street that it took a stranger to point out that there might be a temple underneath!

A caretaker opens a gate in the railings and you descend 40 steps pausing now and then to look across at the temple from different levels. The cornices still retain colouring in some of the carving. By temple standards that of Khnum is small and only the hall remains. When you cross the courtyard and enter, you are in relative darkness after the bright sunlight outside. Surprisingly the roof is complete and is supported by twenty-four columns in six rows with flower capitals of varying design. The carvings on the inner and

Nile scene

outer walls depict various Roman Emperors. When the Romans conquered Egypt they adopted many of the Pharaonic gods and added their own type of artistic work to the temples. The Egyptians carved into the walls which is the reason they could not show figures face-on, whereas the Romans cut in relief. Yet the word relief is commonly used to describe all types of wall carving.

In the hall on the right is a relief of the Emperor Claudius being carried in procession. He is the same Claudius who had the Bible translated into Greek.

The temple of Horus at Edfu

During the Christian era two small chambers were built just inside the facade, one for vestments and the other as a library. A zodiac can just be discerned in the ceiling where soot from sacrificial fires has blackened it. As you walk further back in the hall you return to Pharaonic times. The walls and columns are covered with reliefs of the God Khnum. One shows him being offered sacrifices by Ptolemy IV and, most lovely of all, the God being presented with a large cage of birds decorated with lotus blossoms.

Edfu Temple

The town of Edfu lies equidistant between Luxor and Aswan, 65 miles (105 km) from each. It is a thriving place but is best known for its temple, the best preserved in Egypt. As soon as you dock you find horse-drawn carriages waiting to take you to see it. After a ten minute clip-clop through shop-lined streets you leave your gharry just beyond the town. However, if you wish to buy anything there are the usual vendors at the entrance to entice you.

Although the temple is fairly new, having been built by Ptolemy III, he wisely kept to the designs of the Ramses period a thousand years earlier. It took 180 years to build and a century to carve the reliefs. It was finished as we see it today fifty-seven years before the birth of Christ and dedicated to Horus, the Falcon God, son of Isis and Osiris.

Myths about Horus are many but one explains why his protective wings are on the lintels of pylons and in many tombs. It appears that Horus was asked by the King of the Gods, who had just left Nubia, to quell a revolution there. This Horus did but although he won many skirmishes, the enemy decided to use magic. They turned themselves into crocodiles and hippopotami and infested the Nile in Egypt. So Horus countered with more magic, by assuming the form of a winged disc. This put an end to the trouble and terrified the enemy—still pretending to be hippos and crocodiles–so that they fled back to Nubia (the Sudan) where they remain to this day. The King of the Gods was well satisfied. He ordered Thoth to place carvings of a winged disc in the sanctuaries of temples in Upper and Lower Egypt as a sign of Horus' protection. This may explain why there are no crocodiles in the Egyptian Nile today!

One wonders what Anthony and Cleopatra thought of this lovely building if they ever worshipped there. It must have been finished by the time they took their famous sail on the Nile. It is puzzling also why such a perfect temple should have been ignored and built over. In the cases of Luxor and Denderah, they were in ruins already when people first started to use them as dwellings. Mariette helped keep parts of it free from encroaching sand but did not have enough backing to save it. About the time of the opening of the Suez Canal, parts of the roof were under houses and stables. Those visitors who wished to see it, had to slide down a sand bank and clamber up it again afterwards.

Edfu temple is enormous. 450 feet (137 m) long, its pylon 260 feet (79 m) wide and 115 feet (35 m) high, the clean-cut simplicity adds to its grandeur.

You first enter an open courtyard surrounded by a covered colonnade of thirty-two columns. The rear walls are embellished with carvings. One shows Horus in a boat, sails billowing, catching the leg of a hippopotamus and thrusting a spear into its mouth. For good measure Isis is assisting by holding a rope around the hippo's neck. A colossal statute of Horus in the form of a falcon wearing the double crown of Egypt stands guard on the left side of the entrance, its wings folded. It is made of grey granite, superbly carved and is worth going to see on its own. The facade of the entrance vestibule is the most beautiful part of the building. The doorway is flanked by three columns, the spaces between them filled in to half their height by carved stone screens. The Horus statue waits just in front as if bidding you to enter.

From the vestibule you walk through the hypostyle hall, getting a wonderful view down a further series of halls. These once were closed off by large sycamore doors but now only the hinge sockets remain. Each hall is somewhat smaller than the one behind until you reach the shrine where an altar once supported a golden replica of Horus which is now in the Cairo Antiquities Museum. About its neck there is a blue scarab. Ten chambers surround the sanctuary and one contains a charming relief showing Isis and Osiris embracing one another. On another wall a handsome pharaoh is presenting a vase of wine to Horus, while near him a priest is offering incense. All the well-known Pharaonic signs are here, the Key of Life, the Staff of Happiness and the lotus, divine symbol of resurrection. Unfortunately, many of the faces of the gods and pharaohs are partially obliterated. Christians caused much of this damage in the temples along the Nile during the early Christian era.

There is a circular staircase of 252 steps leading up to the temple roof. It is somewhat hazardous as there are no bannisters and it is dark. The last time I was there it was closed but if you are able to get to the top you can see the perfect symmetry of the temple. Below you, the little town of Edfu stretches to the right with rolling green fields to the left. Straight ahead is the Nile while on the far horizon the gold of the desert melts into the blue sky.

David Roberts, the renowned Scots artist, loved the Middle East and in 1838 he sailed down the Nile, stopping at the various temples to paint them. In his journal he records his visit to Edfu. He found it fascinating and tells of a walk of five miles through fields of maize to reach it. He thought it was the most perfect temple in Egypt and records: 'True it is not of the magnitude of Karnak, nor is it in such good preservation as Denderah but it has one thing they lack. In every situation from which it is viewed it is a picture.' When he returned to his boat, he saw crocodiles sunning themselves on the banks and pigeons were cooing. Perhaps it was the migratory season because he also saw partridge, wild geese and even an eagle. Roberts made another painting of Edfu in 1860. His engravings can sometimes be found to this day, at a price.

Kom Ombo Temple

Kom Ombo temple on the east bank of the river is 100 miles (160 km) south of Luxor. No temple, as seen from the Nile, could be on a better site. It is just round a curve in the river. As our ship made a wide turn it was suddenly before us, its mass of walls and pillars a soft light brown angainst the washed-blue sky of early morning. Below it an apron of green cultivation ended in a line of mimosa trees which edged the water, their branches heavy with yellow blossom. We went ashore and walked along a narrow path through ripening crops. Birds sang merrily. Men were raising water with shadoofs.

The temple was so close that in a few minutes we were within its precincts. It is dedicated to two deities, Sobek the Crocodile God, also venerated in the Fayoum, and Haroeris, God of the Morning Sun. Everything is duplicated to avoid any jealousy. There are two courts, two halls and two sanctuaries. To the right of the entrance, if you glance through railings into a little chapel standing alone and dedicated to Hathor, you will see something you never

Sobek, The Crocodile God, from Ombo Temple

dreamed of before–a pile of mummified crocodiles. They were uncovered in a pit some years ago. Strange to think that at one time they were worshipped! Earrings hung from their ears and bracelets encircled their forepaws. They were fed rich food and the priests held them in great veneration. Now their scales look dusty and ill-kempt. Beyond the walls on the north side there is a large nilometer. It is in the usual form of a well but larger and deeper than the one we saw later on Elephantine Island. Its depth used to be gauged by descending a circular stairway.

The temple, which was excavated in 1833, has high lotus-topped columns and is mostly open to the sky. Traces of colourful Pharaonic design can be seen on the cornice and inside the roof. Reliefs on the walls tell of deeds and wonders and are still legible today. Signs of the fruitfulness of the Nile appear again and again in the form of a figure pouring water from an urn which flows into bread, grapes and flowers. A physician can be seen in his surgery. His instruments are displayed; scissors, scales, spoons, vials of medicine and herbs. Two patients are waiting to see him, one a pregnant woman. Captives are shown tied upside-down to the prows of ships returning from a successful campaign.

A mural several yards long is a line of prisoners each minus an arm and the next relief shows the method of severing the limb. A lion is chewing off the arm of the victim! Next to it, in complete contrast, a priest is pouring water on lotus blossoms as a sacrifice to the gods.

10

ASWAN

Cruising from Kom Ombo to Aswan, always creates a feeling of excitement. Near the town you will find some of the most fascinating things to see on your whole trip. The unique temple of Philae, rescued from the Nile like Abu Simbel; the great High Dam; the famous granite quarries–the list is long. Best of all perhaps is the climate, as heady as a sip of ice-cold champagne. Can it be that it has just that little bit more oxygen than anywhere else? Of course not– but there must be a reason why you always feel ten years younger on arrival.

Aswan, on the east bank of the Nile and some 560 miles (900 km) south of Cairo, is one of the largest towns in Egypt. Parts of it are historic, the rest, which has mushroomed since the building of the Dam, is modern. The best example of this is right along the Nile where you are bound to see it: the Old Cataract Hotel built over a century ago, and its counterpart the New Cataract Hotel, a high rise block alongside it. They share the same beautiful garden and swimming pool.

Your ship ties up among many others next to one of the nicest corniches in Egypt which ends in a curve next to the Cataract hotels. The problem is what to visit first. This may depend on whether you have just completed a cruise or are just about to start one. Certainly, if you are going sightseeing you will need walking shoes, sunglasses and perhaps a sun hat. If you forget to pack the latter you can buy a crushable cotton one anywhere.

The Granite Quarries

The best time to visit the quarries is in the early morning or late afternoon, as there is no shade there. It is only a short distance from the town and on the way you pass an ancient Arab cemetery. The gravestones and mausolea are not of granite strangely enough but of sandstone, purloined long ago from Ptolemaic buildings. The Arabic used on the tomb inscriptions is that in which only the very oldest copies of the Koran are written. These engravings tell that many Muslims were brought for burial from far afield to this carefully selected place. As you drive closer to the quarries the land becomes bare and sandy. Recently, however, trees have been planted near the entrance and a wrought iron gateway leads into the quarries and also keeps the vendors at bay. Once inside you climb a few steps up to the 'unfinished obelisk' and can stand on it. Large chunks of rock sparkle in the sunshine, black, white and varieties of pink. From this spot came furnishings for the great Pharaonic temples. The unfinished obelisk on which you stand is still only partly hewn out of the rock. During the Eighteenth Dynasty while it was being wrought it developed a wide crack down one side. An attempt was made to cut it down to a smaller size but the massive piece of granite proved too flawed. The workmen were told to abandon it and ever since it has lain uncompleted.

The cutting of the granite was a lengthy process. Holes were drilled along the line of the cut and these were filled with wooden pegs. When water was poured on them they expanded and split the rock as required. The monoliths were moved to the nearby Nile on rollers and floated in barges to their destinations. The granite covering over the Pyramid of Mycerinus, the Third Pyramid at Giza, was brought from Aswan in the Fourteenth Dynasty and barges floated others down the river for Pepi I two dynasties later. From these quarries also have come indirectly, gifts to the Western world. The Khedives of Egypt in the last century were very generous. They followed the example set by their forebears when Constantine was given the great obelisk made to honour Thothmes III which now stands in front of St Peter's in Rome.

When Cleopatra fell in love with Anthony she built a temple for him in Alexandria and arranged that two ancient obelisks from Heliopolis should be moved to stand either side of the entrance. One is now in Central Park in New York while the other stands on the Thames embankment in London–Cleopatra's Needle. Both were given over a century ago and both suffered vicissitudes before arriving at their respective destinations. The American one was loaded onto the steamship *Dessouk* after cutting a hole in her bow and arrived safely. The one for London was given in gratitude for ridding Egypt of Napoleon. Although appreciated, it was considered too expensive to move by the British Government. An eminent surgeon of the day, Sir Erasmus Wilson, came to the rescue and paid £10,000 to have it brought to London. For the sea journey it was cased in a steel shell fitted out as a ship with deck and mast. Then began its long voyage in tow but, in a storm off the Spanish coast it broke adrift and tossed and turned for some time. Finally it was taken in tow again by the steamer *Anglia* and reached the Thames during the winter of 1878. It was erected beside the river and greatly admired by the Victorians. It stands on the Thames embankment today flanked by two large sphinxes. For almost 100 years tourists have come to gaze at it and perhaps have their photographs taken sitting between the paws of a sphinx.

The Aga Khan's Mausoleum

The late Aga Khan, spiritual leader of the Ismailis, a Shi'ite sect, died in 1957 and was buried in Aswan. His beautiful mausoleum is a miniature copy of the El Giyushi mosque on the Crags of Cairo's Mokattam Hills. His tomb is also

The Nile at Aswan with the Aga Khan's tomb on the far bank

on a hilltop and is the one place in the world where he wished to be buried. It commands wonderful views in all directions. From dawn to dusk there is a changing panorama: the activity on the river and in the town beyond, the quiet of the desert, the changing colours and the exotic birds in the wiry tamarisk trees, the rising and the setting of the sun. There could not be a more beautiful place for final rest. Pilgrims come from many parts of the world to pay homage and there are streams of tourists every day. You sail across from the east bank in a felucca to get there which only takes a few minutes. You can walk up to it along a winding path with a flight of steps every few yards. On the first flight there is a shopping arcade. Although the views on the way are lovely it is quite a steep, long climb and if you prefer to go on a camel or donkey, there are plenty at the landing stage.

Although the Aga Khan was one of the richest of men (each year he received his weight in diamonds from his followers) he spent most of his life not in palaces but in some of the world's most famous hotels. Hotel managers became his friends and hall porters his *aides-de-camp*, and they were loyal to him. He always kept a suite at the Ritz in London and loved the Old Cataract Hotel in Aswan. He enjoyed the winter months there. He always had the same suite overlooking the Nile whence he could see the top of the hill where, like the pharaohs of old, he built his tomb. At the foot of the hill where the river curves he built his favourite villa, Nur el Salaam, Light of Peace. The Begum, his lovely French wife, still spends some time there in the winter months and, when she is in residence, she places a red rose on his tomb each morning.

The entrance to the mausoleum is up a gleaming rose granite staircase. Before you ascend you must remove your shoes and cameras are not permitted. Large bronze doors swing back to reveal the interior which is open to the sky. It resembles a high courtyard with crenellated edging and is made of pinkish sandstone. The floor is polished rose granite and red carpeting leads across it into a domed inner chamber. Here lies his simple Carrara marble sarcophagus covered in Arabic script.

The Aga Khan loved Mena House Hotel at the foot of the Pyramids and often stayed there. One visit happend to coincide with his jubilee and the Begum had all her jewels with her. The manager arranged for special guards to surround the hotel and its safe was stuffed like Tutankhamun's tomb. The Begum is one of the world's best dressed women and guests peered and gasped whenever she made one of her spectacular appearances. He on the other hand would would walk across to the golf course in his shirt sleeves or an old pullover, his trousers tucked up above his ankles and a crumpled white hat on his head. Golf was a sacred game to him. His handicap varied between eight and ten and he pursued the game with the same enthusiasm that he had for horse racing. He won the Derby five times with his horses but the winning of an open golf championship always eluded him.

One of his good friends was Milo Niederhauser, manager of the Mena House Hotel. Whether the Aga Khan stayed there or not he always paid a call at the hotel to say hello to Milo and before he left Cairo he went again to say goodbye.

Botanic Island

When Lord Kitchener was Consul General in Egypt, his two hobbies were collecting antique books and studying flowers and trees. He often ran valuable second-hand books to earth in the Khan el Khalili in Cairo and, to his delight, he was presented with an island in the Nile at Aswan now known as Botanic Island. Here he could indulge his hobby of plant collecting. In a short time, once this passion became known, he received gifts of exotic plants and trees from many countries. Today we can enjoy this lovely island where many experiments are carried out and trees and flowers flourish.

Botanic Island is perfect for walking and has a pathway right across it lined with flowers and overhead trellises. Many of the specimens are labelled. There are stalls where you can buy such things as bead and nut necklaces and other souvenirs. A small rustic café sells cooling drinks and there are all kinds of exotic birds. A visit to the island is often combined into one felucca trip with that to the Aga Khan's tomb on the far bank. While at the latter it is only a short walk beyond the mausoleum to go and see an old Coptic monastery built during the twelfth century and dedicated to St Simeon. The living quarters of the monks and their church are in ruins but recognizable.

Returning to Botanic Island you go ashore up a flight of steps from your boat through a mass of bougainvillea and then it is flowers all the way. Your felucca will sail round the island and await you at the far end. This walk through the lush tropical garden with so many things growing that are new to European eyes is a novel experience. One of the things about a sunny predictable climate is the way plants waiting to be set out remind one of a greenhouse. They are in pots stacked on dried mud shelves of different heights, all in various stages of growth but without benefit of glass enclosures.

I asked a gardener about a plant of the mimosa type but with blue flowers, which interested me. He told me that, if I put my hands towards it, it would shrink away from them. It did so and I quickly withdrew them whereupon it slowly rose up and looked beautiful again. It was indeed a species of mimosa with mauve-blue flowers, *leguminosae* for the experts, I understand, but the touch-me-not plant to most of us.

Elephantine Island

This island is 1½ miles (2.5 km) long in the centre of the river opposite the town. It is full of interest with something for everyone: some Pharaonic temple remains, a village, one of the most famous nilometers in Egypt, paths, trees and, keeping the punchline until last, a de luxe Oberoi hotel which provides a regular ferry service to the town using pseudo-Pharaonic boats.

The Nile is particularly lovely at Aswan with its islands, shore scenery and dark grey rocks. Elephantine Island indeed is so named because of its rocky

Nile Cataract and feluccas, Aswan

shore at the southern end resembles a herd of elephants standing in the shallows.

The ancient nilometer is attractive and, although not used these days, still works. It consists of a well in which the water rises to exactly the same height as in the river. On the walls are Greek and Demotic scale markings to indicate the water level.

Elephantine Island was not regarded as sacred in the same way as Philae, yet it was venerated. The ancient Egyptians, despite their long journeys into Nubia, knew nothing of the real source of the Nile and firmly believed it was close to Elephantine. A bas-relief illustrating this tenet can be seen in the temple of Isis on its new island. It shows a mass of granite rocks piled high on top of one another surmounted by a hawk and a vulture. The God of the Nile kneels beneath them protected in the coil of a snake. He has a papyrus plant on his head and holds two vases of water. One is slender with a steady stream of water pouring forth while from the other water is gushing more quickly.

At one time there was a great temple to Khnum the ram-headed God on the island. Begun in early times it was added to for centuries down to the Ptolemaic era. Excavations are continually unearthing interesting objects from the ruins. I was fortunate on one visit there to see a newly found statue waiting to be removed to a museum. It had been placed in a small chamber 20 feet (6 m) below ground. It was late afternoon and the sun was slanting down into the excavations, lighting up the side of the broken wall where the little statue sat. For thousands of years it had been blanketed by sand and rubble in complete darkness but this day the sun warmed its body and, with its hands clasped on its knees, it seemed blissfully content absorbing the rays of Amen-Ra himself.

It was from Elephantine that the pharaohs of the Fifth Dynasty sprang. Situated just below the first cataract it was referred to by the Egyptians as the Door to the South. Beyond the Egyptian border it was known as the Key of Egypt. It was governed by powerful nobles whose leader took the title 'Keeper of the Door to the South'. They were rich caravan traders and the pharaohs wisely entrusted them with the defence of the region. Ruthless and strong, no one dared rise against them and riches poured into their domain in the form of slaves, gold, ostrich feathers, ebony, skins and ivory. When barter was necessary, it was a simple matter to procure granite from the Aswan quarries. The old Egyptian word for gold is Nub, and as most of the gold came from south of the border, the country there became known as Nubia.

In dynastic times, the rainfall was plentiful on Elephantine. Fig trees and grape vines kept their leaves throughout the year. There is no cultivation near the ruins today but you can infer how fertile it must have been from the greenery in other parts of the island.

The little museum, a converted villa, has less than half a dozen rooms and is close to the nilometer. The finds are mostly from about 4000 B.C. with some from the Graeco-Roman period. They include small items such as hand mirrors, necklaces of semi-precious stones, scarabs and earrings. The most impressive piece is the top part of a mummified ram, its head and chest covered with gold and with golden straps around its shoulders. The God Khnum was the deity of the first cataract and a sacred ram was symbolic of the god on earth. It was selected from its fellows with as much care as is given to the Dalai Lama when he is chosen from the children of Tibet. The ram, attended by priests, then led a cloistered life in the temple. At death it was mummified and laid in a sarcophagus with rites appropriate to a pharaoh. One horn and the tail were wrapped separately from the body. Gold encased the mummy and around its neck was hung a garland of bay leaves. It was believed that the ram would eventually be reunited with Khnum in the life beyond life.

The rulers of Elephantine were buried on the west bank on a high ridge. Here there is a frieze of dynastic tombs rather like those at Beni Hassan. The indication of their whereabouts is a domed sheik's tomb of recent vintage. They are hewn out of a rock opening onto a terrace. They can be reached by climbing a steep staircase next to a sarcophagus slide which looks rather like a ski-run in the sand.

An intriguing history attaches to tomb 22, that of Herukhuf, a traveller of great repute. His first journey had been by order of King Mer-an-Ra to open up a road in the Sudan in the country of Aam. His second journey is considered to have been a success for he brought back abundant Sudanese produce. Subsequently he led a raiding party deep into Aam and returned with 300 asses laden with myrrh, ebony, oil, grain, ivory and leopard skins. Chieftains on his route, fearful of his great power, sent him gifts of sheep and cattle.

When Pepi II ascended the throne, Heruhkuf was sent on yet another journey. On his way back he sent word to the Pharaoh, who was little more than a youth, that he was bringing many things of interest with him including a pygmy. The latter fired the imagination of the young Pharaoh as pygmies were seldom seen and, if one was obtained, he was expected to be a sort of jester and keep people amused. The Pharaoh was delighted and sent the following missive on papyrus to Herukhuf.

'When he embarketh with thee in the boat then shalt thou appoint trustworthy servants to be about him and on each side of the boat and take heed that he falleth not into the water. When he sleepeth at night appoint also trustworthy servants who shall sleep by his side in his sleeping place and they shall visit him ten times during the night—once every hour. For my Majesty wisheth to see the pygmy more than the tribute of Sinai or Punt. If thou reachest my capital and this pygmy shall be with thee alive and in good health and content, my Majesty will do for thee a greater thing than that which was done for the chancellor of the God Ba-ur-tet in the time of Kin Assa, in the greatness of the heartfelt wish of my Majesty to see this pygmy.'

So Herukhuf brought the pygmy to the Pharaoh at Memphis to dance before his Majesty's august presence. So much did Herukhuf treasure the papyrus from the Pharaoh that he commanded the contents to be carved on the outside of his tomb where you can still see it today.

The Hotel Aswan Oberoi on Elephantine Island is the Shangri-La you dream about: quiet, restful and luxurious. Its duplexes and 150 bedrooms leave nothing to be desired, from mini-bar to perfect service. The rounded swimming pool is of turquoise mosaic and the garden perfect for strolling. The only noise is the singing of birds for there are no cars—not even a Rolls Royce. The scene is constantly changing as it does while you cruise on the Nile for the river surrounds it and feluccas await your pleasure. Beyond the garden are many places to walk. There is the small village and of course the museum. When you arrive at the quay, staff with luggage carts see that you have nothing to carry up to the hotel. There is a shop in the lobby where you can get anything from papyrus paintings to kaftans. A fountain plays on a terrace between one part of the hotel and the other. There is a fully equipped health

A bend in the Nile at Aswan

centre with its own pool offering all the latest treatments and exercises. A novelty to some will be sand baths which are supposed to help cure arthritic complaints. You are buried in warm sand up to the waist and the sun gives you the treatment right down to your toes.

If you feel energetic, duck shoots can be arranged from December to March–with no limit on the bag. In a few minutes you can be in the city by boarding one of the hotel boats. Famous people come and go: Jacques Cousteau's team stayed there while photographing exotic fish in the Nile; politicians and film stars arrive in search of a little peace and quiet. The General Manager, Ibrahim Dessouki, seems to be everywhere and anticipates everyone's needs. He knows Jehan Sadat's favourite dishes, the suite a celebrity particularly likes. His ready smile dissolves anxiety, even when the important telephone call fails to materialize.

You know how much good your stay at the hotel has done you when you have forgotten the date and time and suddenly realize you have to leave tomorrow–but then what do you expect of a Shangri-La?

The increase in the size of Aswan since the construction of the High Dam has in turn produced more shops, many of them along the corniche. There is also a market further back in the town where you can buy all sorts of souvenirs from bead necklaces to carved walking sticks. Aswan has been laid waste in turn by Persians, Turks, Arabs and Nubians, yet nothing quelled its growth due to the strategic position it occupies near the first cataract of the Nile.

It was well known for its wines during the reigns of the Ptolemies; the Greeks mistakenly thought it was on the Tropic of Cancer. It was said that on one day in the year the sun shone vertically down a well, illuminating it in every part so that you could not see the water level. Much of Aswan's wealth came from the gold mines in the Bisharin country.

The Bisharin people are related to the Abyssinians and have changed little down the centuries. Well known for their dancing and singing they also have the most distinctive coiffures. The men's hair stands out in a frizzy cloud while the women plait their own in many thin strings. They are to be seen in the streets of Aswan today where they come to sell various kinds of basketwork and large circular wicker trays hung with shells. Tourists buy them for wall decoration or for serving canapes.

Before visiting the new High Dam, it is interesting to look at the old one on the way, as it was a great achievement in its day. It is some seven miles south of the town. As you cross it you look down at the sluices through which water is thundering. Away to the right the sun sparkles over Aswan. A honey-coloured mosque can be seen in the foreground behind which the town fans out in a labyrinth of buildings, many high-rise flats and offices. It is difficult to remember that this modern place nestling in a fertile curve of the Nile is surrounded by savage desert.

Turn away from the flying spray with its rainbow and face south upstream and you have the contrasting calm of the reservoir behind the dam. Here not long ago you would have seen the half submerged remains of Trajan's temple, often called Pharaoh's Bed, and the Temple of Isis standing on what was once the island of Philae. In Pharaonic times, tradition believed this island to be one of the burial places of Osiris. The ground was so sacred that only priests and temple attendants were allowed to live there. A number of religious plays were presented each year including the mutilation, death and resurrection of Osiris. Great crowds were drawn annually to Philae for this religious ceremony and the island became known as the Pearl of Egypt.

In the early days of Christianity, the Copts built two churches in honour of St Michael and St Athanasius on Philae and remains of other churches and Pharaonic temples were excavated there down through the years. The High Dam construction was going to raise the water level between the two dams and completely submerge the temple remains. It was decided to remove them to a higher site where they could once again be viewed in their entirety before the High Dam was finished.

Philae Temple

The Abu Simbel temples had been salvaged from the river successfully, why not those on Philae? Once again UNESCO and engineers got together to solve the problem. As Philae was already partly submerged by the waters behind the Old Dam, it was necessary to put a coffer dam round the island and pump the water out so that the complete buildings could be removed.

I was in Egypt in 1975 and joined a party of French tourists to see how the work was progressing. I wrote in my diary for that day 'We chugged out to the coffer dam, tied up to a wooden platform and climbed a ladder to the top where we stood on the rubble filling between the two rows of sheet piling which form the dam. A complete circle enclosed the island like an enormous pie dish with currugated edges. Below on the grey soil stood the temples like miniature toys in a large bowl. Over half a century in water had turned the

Philae Temple removed to its island site near Aswan

walls from their once dark apricot colour to the same grey as the drowned land itself. Pumps were still working but much of the island was above the water line.' Many months of work lay ahead: each temple block had to be numbered and then the buildings dismantled to be moved to the island of Agilka, 500 yards long and 160 yards across (470 x 150 m). This island was reshaped to make it a replica of Philae. It lies in the Nile half way between Aswan and the new High Dam, fortunately only 500 yards from the original one. The reconstruction was carried out with the same meticulous care as the Abu Simbel temples and today you can visit Agilka and judge the miracle for yourself.

Unfortunately the colouring has washed away but there are records of it in several books. One reads 'The colours in the ten-columned court and some of the adjacent chambers are of marvellous freshness. The capitals are vivid blue and green picked out with red, crimson and orange. The roof is bright blue with golden stars.'

To visit Agilka and see the temples, your bus or taxi takes you to a landing stage on the east bank of the lake formed between the dams. From there it is a short motor boat ride. You soon see the lovely Isis temple—to the west of it is Hadrian's Gateway (119-138 A.D.) and to the east there is the temple of Hathor. Further beyond there are the fourteen pillars of Pharaoh's Bed. The latter is charming, a Graeco-Roman kiosk erected by Trajan.

Pharoah's Bed, Philae. Submerged at the old site

Walking towards the Isis temple, which is the largest one, you will see that it is an elegant example of the lighter type of architecture favoured in the Ptolemaic era and does not imitate the colossal grandeur seen in the Theban temples. The first pylon is 59 feet (18 m) high. On its facade are reliefs of Pharaoh Ptolemy Neos Dionysos smiting his enemies in the presence of Isis, Horus and Hathor. The pylon has a staircase to the top which is not generally known. If you wish to have a lovely view or take photographs it is worth the climb, if you can arrange it. The colonnade on the east side is unfinished. On the west side of the large courtyard there is a mammisi (house of birth) surrounded by a portico; above the walls the columns have capitals of varying floral designs.

In the small Hathor temple there are musical scenes with the cheerful little god Bes playing a lute and in another dancing with a tambourine. Some scholars say that this jolly fellow is a pygmy figure, some find him ugly–but at least he is amusing and happy.

Before the original island of Philae was submerged it had many trees surrounding the ruins. Acacia and palm trees have been planted on Agilka since the move and already the island is beginning to present the aspect which earlier pictures gave of Philae.

Kalabsha Temple

Kalabsha was the second largest temple in Nubia, built by Augustas Caesar about 27 B.C. and dedicated to the god Mandoulis. As well as the priceless temples at Abu Simbel and Philae, the lake forming behind the High Dam threatened lesser known sites in Nubia such as Kalabsha, Kertassi and Beit el Wali. All three were therefore moved some 31 miles (50 km) north to a promontory just south of the dam on the west bank.

At Kalabsha the pylon, its decorations weatherworn, leads into the usual open court colonnaded on three sides. It has a 50 foot (15m) deep nilometer. This courtyard leads again to a smaller one and, although the reliefs are also indistinct, the columns retain their lotus and papyrus capitals. Three roofed halls at the rear of the temple are in better repair and here you see the king presenting gifts and making obeisance to the deities.

Kertassi, five minutes walk along a stone path with benches, commands magnificent views over the High Dam. The temple is really a delightful kiosk dedicated by the Romans to the goddess Hathor. Nearby Beit el Wali is small also, surprisingly so because it was erected by Ramses II and also honours Hathor. Despite its size it sings the same song about Ramses' great victories, only this time the reliefs are in proportion so that you do not have to stand back to get the right perspective. He is in his chariot with his lion loping beside it, just about to release an arrow from his bow. On the other side of the first open courtyard he is seen on a throne with tributes being presented to him: panther skins, shields, myrrh, ivory, ostrich eggs and feathers. More entrancing are the live animals being given which include monkeys, ibex, panthers, oxen and, most delightful of all, a baby giraffe.

The forecourt leads into a hall with thin fluted pillars and on to the sanctuary where the wall facing you has two niches each containing an identical trio of statues, the foremost one a deified Ramses flanked by two gods. The colouring is vivid and unexpected after the drowned temples. Offerings are being presented and the bodies of the pharaohs and gods are pink as if alive. Their robes and jewels are bright reds, blues and yellows. If you visit these temples, do not miss this one because, more than anywhere else, it will give you an idea of how the great temples must have appeared before their colouring vanished.

Aswan High Dam

Among the greatest engineering achievements of the twentieth century is the building of the High Dam at Aswan. It is one of the three largest dams in the world, the work of the descendants of the builders of the Pyramids. I was taken to see it during its construction. My visit was at night since work carried on 24 hours a day. As we approached the site the moon and stars were hanging out of the sky, but as we got closer, a vast cloud of rising dust blotted them out. We left our vehicles, walked over to some railings and peered down into Dante's Inferno. The Nile had been diverted so that the foundations could be anchored to the rock. The whole project was floodlit and hundreds of men, using the full panoply of modern earth-moving equipment, were working away far below like a huge colony of ants. The noise made conversation impossible so that it was only after we left that we were able to be given the statistics of the undertaking as you see it today. 4000 yards (3600 m) long, average height 360 feet (111 m), width at the base 590 feet (180 m) and at the top where there is a double carriageway, 131 feet (40 m). Lake Nasser, now held back by the dam, reaches over 300 miles (486 km) south into the Sudan. Thousands of villagers had to be moved from the area and rehoused. The presence of this large body of water is changing the climate in Aswan, which now occasionally gets rain that it never had previously.

The lake acts as a settling basin and the fertile mud which the Nile used to carry the length of Egypt and even out into the Mediterranean is now deposited above the dam. In the distant future Lake Nasser may even silt up. It is a sobering thought that Man now has the ability to interfere with nature on such an enormous scale.

The generators are contained within the dam itself and all you can see are the huge jets of escaping water on the downstream side, often crowned with rainbows. The electricity generated is carried by ultra high voltage lines for distribution throughout Egypt and should supply its needs for some time to come.

Construction of the Aswan Dam

11

LAKE NASSER
AND
ABU SIMBEL

The two most popular monuments to see in Egypt are the Pyramids and Abu Simbel and fate has decreed that they should be almost as far apart as possible, one in Cairo and the other at the furthest stretch of Upper Egypt on Lake Nasser.

The Nile cruises stop at Aswan and from there the quickest and easiest way to go to Abu Simbel is by an EgyptAir flight. There are several each day and it is quite feasible to do the round trip in the day. There are, however, two alternatives which will become available fairly soon. A road is being made along the western shore of the lake which will eventually reach all the way down to the Sudan, passing Abu Simbel on the way. The distance from Aswan is some 180 miles (292 km) so an early start and late return by car or bus will become practicable.

The second possibility will almost certainly be to cruise south to the temple and visit it from a boat/hotel just as you do now in the lower reaches of the Nile. At one time there was a hydrofoil service from Aswan but this no longer operates. There are steamers on the lake which carry local passengers down to the Sudan but they are not luxury cruisers. The lock system which bypasses the dam is not big enough to handle the cruise boats so they cannot get onto the lake. However, the construction of cruise boats on the lake just above the dam is being considered and, when and if this happens, it will certainly become the best alternative of all. At present there is only one small hotel at Abu Simbel and so the use of cruise boats would change the whole situation. In addition, the presence of cruise boats on the lake would undoubtedly open it up for tourism in due course. Already a leisure complex, Tat Amun, just south of the dam is nearly complete at the time of writing (1985) which will offer all the water sports and, it is hoped, golf and tennis–surely a taste of things to come.

Abu Simbel Temples

The temples of Abu Simbel are on the west bank of the Nile. Burckhardt came across them in 1817 and, when the news reached Cairo, it caused great excitement. Part of the facade was covered with wind blown sand and it was decided to uncover it. Belzoni was sent from Cairo to look into the matter but somehow the project did not materialize, probably because of the great distance from the capital.

David Roberts wished to paint Abu Simbel and found it still in the same deplorable condition. Having made sketches of the facade, like Burckhardt before him, he managed to get inside the temple and reached the sanctuary where he found four seated statues facing an altar. They were of Ramses II and three gods, Ptah, Amun and Re-Hamarchis. He wrote up his diary on the altar and while doing so lamented the finding of so much graffiti everywhere except on the alter itself. He did not realize that even Belzoni had cut his name in bold letters on the inner side of the alter. However Roberts was to play a prank on this theme. In his lithograph of this facade, he inscribed his name on the leg of one of the statues and that of Muhammad on another!

In later decades the temple was carefully dug out of the engulfing sand as more and more travellers went to visit it, and so it regained its magnificence. Ironically, with the coming of the High Dam it looked as if it would be engulfed once more, this time by water.

The saving of Abu Simbel is proof, if any was needed, of what international co-operation can achieve. The project was mounted under the general direction of UNESCO and much has been written about it. Behind the temple

Abu Simbel being reassembled

Abu Simbel Temple re-erected on its new site

and higher up, a site duplicating the original was created where it would be above the new water line. What appears to you today as a solid background is in fact an artificial hill. The huge blocks comprising the temples and statues were numbered, cut with special diamond toothed saws and lifted by cranes to an intermediate resting place to await re-erection. Rush matting screens were used to protect the colours from the glare of the sun.

In common with many other visitors I saw it in this transitional stage. I remember looking into a section of one of the giant Ramses' faces as it sat on the sand. The upper part of the eyeballs were curved more than the lower to give the correct perspective when the face was atop its 65 foot (20 m) figure and viewed from below. A nearby ear had a pierced lobe for earrings, the hole so large you could put your foot throught it.

As you circle in to land at Abu Simbel the clear blue of the water looks enticing. When you descend the outlines of the temples become clearer: that of Nefertari, Ramses' favourite wife, lies beside the much taller one of the great Pharaoh. The four seated statues of Ramses patiently await your arrival. You almost feel as if one of the figures might raise a hand in welcome.

You land at a small airstrip behind the monuments and in a few minutes a bus takes you beyond the Nefertari Hotel, past some houses, gardens and a swimming pool to the temple site. The Ramses statues are impassive and gaze

Horus statues at the feet of one of the Ramses statues at Abu Simbel

Nefertari Temple at Abu Simbel

into space quite unimpressed by the fact that it recently cost £15 million to move them. Above them are inscribed the names and titles of the greatest Pharaoh. A row of monkeys worshipping the sunrise is carved on top. Smaller statues of the different members of the royal family stand to the right and left and between the great feet.

Going through the entrance you are in a hall 56 feet (17 m) by 52 feet (16 m) with eight columns. On either side are 33 foot (10 m) statues of the King dressed as Osiris. The roof depicts the sky with large birds hovering between constellations of stars. The walls show, on the left, the Pharaoh making obeisance to various deities and, on the right, scenes of his Kadesh victory. Eight chambers open off this hall to right and left, and straight ahead is a further hall with four pillars. Here Ramses and Nefertari are making offerings to yet more gods. You pass through another hall into the sanctuary.

Reliefs illuminated at night in the Nefertari Temple

The length of the temple from the facade is 200 feet (61 m) and the architecture was so exact that twice a year at the equinoxes the rising sun strikes straight down into the sanctuary and floods the statues with its rays.

A few yards away to the north of the Ramses temple is the one he built for Nefertari which is dedicated to Hathor. Its facade is much smaller and has statues each in a separate niche: four of Ramses, two of his wife and some smaller ones of their children. The hall has six pillars with Hathor capitals. The reliefs here depict peaceful rather than warlike pursuits. Murals of Nefertari show her to be as beautiful as Nefertiti. Her royal robes are cut on simple lines in transparent pleated linen. In one lovely picture she is presenting offerings to Anuket, Goddess of the First Cataract, the latter wearing an enchanting crown of lotus flowers. Unfortunately history does not tell us much about Nefertari, but she was obviously a fascinating creature. Her tomb is in the Valley of the Queens where the reliefs are in the same attractive vein.

Appendix 1
List of 4 and 5 Star Hotels
Classification by Egyptian Tourist Office

Cairo

5 star		Tel.
El Salaam Hyatt	61 Abdel Hamid Badawi Street, Heliopolis	867176
Holiday Inn	Alexandria Desert Road, Pyramids	852266
Sonesta	4 El Tarayan Street, Nasr City	609444
Mena House Oberoi	Al Ahram Street, Pyramids	853789
Meridien	Corniche el Nil	845444
Nile Hilton	Tahrir Square	740777
Ramses Hilton	Corniche el Nil	740777
Sheraton Cairo	Galaa Bridge	983000
Sheraton Heliopolis	Airport Road, Heliopolis	665500
Sheraton Tower	Gezira	
Shepheards	Corniche el Nil	33800
Marriott	30 Hassan Assem Street, Zamalek	819918
Siag Pyramids Penta	59 Maryutiya, Sakkara Road	856007

4 star		
Atlas	2 Bank el Gomhoria Street	918311
Atlas Zamalek	20 Gamet el Dowal el Arabia	800645
Concorde	Cairo Airport	690077
Cairo International Airport	Cairo Airport	966074
Cleopatra	Tahrir Square	759945
El Borg	Saray el Gezira Street	816068
El Nil	Ahmed Ragab Street, GardenCity	22805
Joliville	Alexandria Desert Road,Pyramids	855510
Manial Palace	El Manial Street	844535
Radisson Oasis	Alexandria Desert Road	851506
Baron Metropole	Ma'ahad el Sahary Street	669005
El Maadi	Main Entrance, Maadi	635896
Green Pyramids	Helmeyet El Ahram Street	852600
Holiday Inn Sphinx	Alexandria Desert Road, Pyramids	854700
Novotel	Cairo Airport	661330

Alexandria

5 star		Tel.
Palestine	Montazah Palace	861687
Sheraton	(under construction)	

4 star		
Al Salamlek	Montazah Palace	860585
Beau Rivage	443 Al Guesh Avenue	62185
Cecil	16 Saad Zaghloul Square	867005
El Alamein	Sidi Abdel Rahman	807532
Maamura Palace	Maamura	865401
San Stefano	Al Guesh Avenue	63580
Windsor	117 El Shuhada Street	808700
Alexandria	23 El Nasr Square, El Mansheya	801041
Al haram	163 El Gueish Street, Cleopatra	963984

Luxor

5 star		Tel.
Etap	Al Nil Street	2011
New Winter Palace	Al Nil Street	2222
4 star		
Movenpick Jolie Ville	Crocodile Island	83400
Isis	Khalid Ibn el Walid Street	2750
Savoy	Al Nil Street	2200
Akhnaton Hotel Village	Luxor	777575

Aswan

5 star		Tel.
New Cataract	Abtal el Tahrir Street	3222
Oberoi	Elephantine Island	3455
4 star		
Amun	Amun Island	2555
Cataract	Abdel el Tahrir Street	2233
Kalabsha	Abdel el Tahrir Street	2999

Hurgada

4 star		Tel.
Sheraton	Hurgada	785

Appendix 2
List of Nile Cruise Ships

Name	Operator	No. of Cabins
Ani	Sheraton	76
Aton	Sheraton	76
Hotep	Sheraton	76
Isis	Hilton	48

Osiris	Hilton	48
Lindblad Explorer	Salen Lindblad Cruising	—
Lindblad Polaris	Salen Lindblad Cruising	—
Marriott Flair	Marriott Hotel Co.	57
Nile Beauty	Egyptian Co. for Floating Hotels	50
Nile Concorde	Fluvial Tourism & Hotel Co.	45
Nile Emperor	Presidential Nile Cruises	70
Nile President	Presidential Nile Cruises	60
Nile Princess	Nile Princess Co.	31
Nile Sphinx	Sphinx Tours Co.	50
Reve Vacane	Sphinx Tours Co.	20
Seti First	Magdy George Hassanein	54
Seti Second	Magdy George Hassanein	37
Sphinx	Sphinx Tours Co.	20
Triton	Trans Egypt Travel	47
Tut	Sheraton	82
Araba	Middle East Floating Hotels Co.	38
		3 suites
El Karnak	Pyramids Tours Co.	22
King Tut Fleet (NISR)	Cairo Hotel & Fluvial Tourism Ltd.	
Nile Star	Eastmar Tours Co.	40
Pyramids	Pyramids Tours Co.	22
Queen Cleopatra	Pyramids Tours Co.	18
Queen Nefertiti	Pyramids Tours Co.	22
Ramses	Pyramids Tours Co.	18
Tutankhamun	Pyramids Tours Co.	18
El Salam	Gayed Co. for Fluvial Boats	40
Memphis	Eastmar Tours Co.	21
Nefertari	Eastmar Tours Co.	42
Neptune	Trans Egypt Travel	58
Nile Explorer	Gabsun Fluvial Tourism Co.	20
Admiral Prince	Amir Zaky Diab	30
Amon	Fluvial Tourism Hotels Co.	20
Aswan	Abercrombie & Kent	11
Abu Simbel	Abercrombie & Kent	11
Champoleon	Mediterranean Co.	40
Horis	International Co. for Fluvial Tourism	58
Khufu	Pyramids Tours Co.	6
Memnon	Nesim S. Mansour	13
Nile Dream	Internile Co. for Floating Hotels & Tourism	45
Rania	VIP Co.	
Sarah	Sarah Tours	20
Shadiah	VIP Co.	22

Subek	Abdel Aty	11
Sultana	VIP Co.	25
Tut	Fluvial Tourism & Hotel Co.	20
Abis	FluvialNavigation Co.	20
Golden Boat	International Nile Cruise	50

Appendix 3
Useful words in Arabic spelt phonetically for pronunciation

Yes	Aiwa	Bring me	Hatli
No	La	Here	Henna
How much	Becalm	Listen	Isma
Good day	Sa-eeda	I do not have	Mafeesh
Never mind	Marleesh	Taxi	Taxi
Please	Menfadlak	Bus	Autobus
Thank you	Shookrarn	Good	Kwice
Stop	Stanner shwyer	Milk	Layban
Little	Shwyer	Sugar	Sooker
Possible	Moomkin	Tea	Shy
Not Possible	Moosh Moomkin	Coffee	Ahwa
That's all	Bus	Water	Moya
Right	Yemeen	Street	Sharia
Left	Shemarn	Village	Ezba
Money	Feloose	If God is willing	
Give me	Eddeenie	often used for 'yes')	In sharla

Appendix 4
Arabic numerals

1	Wahid	١		6	Sitta	٦
2	Eckneen	٢		7	Sarba	٧
3	Talata	٣		8	Tamanya	٨
4	Arba	٤		9	Tessa	٩
5	Khamsa	٥		10	Ashra	١٠

Appendix 4
A The Hieroglyphic Alphabet
B Some Pharaonic Symbols

SOME PHARAONIC SYMBOLS.

CROOK

SCEPTRE

FLAIL

KEY OF LIFE

DOUBLE CROWN

CARTOUCHE

THE HIEROGLYPHIC ALPHABET

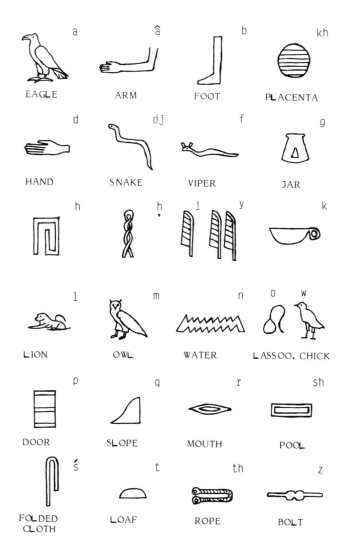

Index